# THE FISCAL CLIFF
How the Trump Presidency Can Save America's Declining
Cities

# THE FISCAL CLIFF
## The Financial Crisis Facing American Cities

By:
## EDWARD POTEAT

# TABLE OF CONTENT

# INTRODUCTION

The seeds of the most beautiful flower are worthless unless those seeds are planted in soil that can nurture the growth and development of that seed. So a rose is simply a byproduct of strong roots planted in firm soil. Communities work in much the same way. Cities that are unable to meet the rudimentary needs of its citizens rob its young and most defenseless people of their basic rights. These residents are forced to live half-lives with poor education, poor health care, diminished options for a successful adult life, and a higher probability of incarceration. These declining cities do not have the resources to deliver quality health care, quality public education, or decent housing, and they put their citizens at a distinct disadvantage. I should know. I grew up in a declining city.

New York City in 2016 is a far different place than New York City in the 1980's. Today, crime is at an all-time low, and the city has a diverse economy driven by growth industries such as financial services and media. But in the 1980's, New York City was slowly recovering from the fiscal crisis of the 1970's. Manufacturing, which was a leading industry then, was in sharp decline; the crack epidemic stretched an already thin police force; and the decline in population left many neighborhoods with empty buildings and vacant commercial corridors. Between just 1950 and 1980, New York City lost more than one million people.

As a teenager, I had a diverse group of friends. I grew up in East Harlem but was familiar with kids from all over the City, including the tony Upper East Side. Although East

Harlem and the Upper East Side are adjoining neighborhoods and only separated by 96th Street, they are vastly different. The Upper East Side has some of the wealthiest zip codes in the country. While east Harlem has suffered from poor educational facilities, poverty, an overconcentration of public housing, and health care indicators like asthma that are commensurate with developing countries.

I often crossed over 96th Street by foot as I made my way home after hanging out with my friends. As I walked, I noticed that the amount of garbage in the road and on the sidewalk increased. The Upper East Side did not have any abandoned buildings, while that was a common sight in East Harlem. In fact, the most famous landmark in East Harlem was an ugly, elevated train line running along Park Avenue. This was the same Park Avenue that the super-rich on the Upper East Side lived on, but half a mile uptown in East Harlem, things looked quite different.

Although the disparities in these neighborhoods were obvious, the reasons behind these disparities were less so. I simply believed, like most of my friends and neighbors, the city's bureaucracy chose to ignore our problems. The conspicuous drug trafficking on our corners could easily be addressed by positioning a larger police force in the neighborhood. The disparity in public schools could easily be solved with increased funding. And the gross disparity in health care options could be fixed through more generous funding to our hospitals. My friends on the Upper East Side benefitted from their socioeconomic status as members of White and wealthy families, but my family's and my immediate neighbors' socio-economic status as working-class Black and Latino families allowed the government bureaucrats to ignore our condition.

As an adult, I've spent a great deal of my professional life addressing the disparity between poor communities of color and wealthier ones. I've worked with countless community development corporations, churches, and not-for-profit organizations to create affordable housing throughout New York City. In a small way, my developments have chipped away at the inequality between the poor and rich by providing decent and new housing to poor individuals. I am proud of these accomplishments, but I remain frustrated by the growing and persistent disparity between poor and rich households.

The willful neglect of poor communities of color is a real and clear phenomenon throughout the United States. My story as a teenager growing up in an impoverished community of color has been recounted many times in movies, articles, and even music. However, I've come to realize that another factor besides willful neglect causes municipalities to make these harmful decisions. Societal ills associated with the inner city like the lack of proper health care, proper public education or decent housing are just symptoms of a deeper problem. Certain cities or declining cities are not unwilling to address these concerns. They are unable to because they cannot afford to !!!

I, like many liberal leaning Democrats, was initially dismayed when Donald Trump became the 45th President of the United States. However, I now realize that a Trump Presidency may truly represent a new start for America's inner cities and declining cities.

The Great Recession of 2008 laid bare the truth that many cities cannot fund the delivery of the most basic of services to its citizens. Several cities in California including San Bernardino and Stockton have already filed bankruptcy. And municipal bankruptcies are not limited to California. Jefferson County, the home of Birmingham, Alabama, filed bankruptcy in 2011. In the fall of 2013, Detroit became the largest city in the country to ever file bankruptcy.

Exactly what are basic services cities should give to its' citizens? Every resident of a city pays taxes so that the city can provide health care through its hospital system; safety through its police and firefighters; sanitation through its sanitation and sewer departments; and education through its schools. Municipalities are supposed to provide these basic services to its citizens. But newspapers and magazine articles are littered with stories about cities that are cutting back on their police forces, social services, and hospital and public education systems. These cutbacks have the greatest impact on poor communities that rely on the government for these services.

While many books have documented the symptoms of declining cities, *The Fiscal Cliff* addresses the problem head on. The symptoms of declining cities such as poor health care, poor schools, and a diminishing public safety apparatus are the most obvious manifestations. While many authors have identified these symptoms as the central problem and have attempted to find solutions for them, I argue that these issues seem intractable because they are not the problem but only the symptoms. Although poverty and the disastrous effects of poverty exist throughout America, these problems are compounded by declining cities.

The term Fiscal Cliff has been made famous by the inability of our Congress to avoid debilitating arguments over the budget for the federal government. However, the fiscal cliff facing many American municipalities is more serious and unavoidable. Declining cities have cut spending and increased taxes for years since they are mandated to balance their budgets annually. However, they cannot cut services further without hurting their clients or citizens that need these services or without alienating their clients / citizens through increased taxes.

Although significant time will be spent discussing the nature and definition of a declining city in the book, I'll cursory define declining cities here. In short, declining cities are cities that have suffered from a significant loss in population and economic base. Since the infrastructure of any city is fairly static, a city with a declining population has a bloated infrastructure comprised of abandoned houses, hospitals, and schools. Once the parameters of a declining city are defined, the book will discuss various solutions to address the problems facing them.

For example, Baltimore City is a classic example of a declining city. Although the infrastruction of Baltimore city (i.e. housing, health care facilities, and educational facilities ) was originally built for a city of nearly 1 million people, Baltimore currently has approximately 600,000 and continues to lose population annually. The evidence of the bloated infrastructure of Baltimore can be seen everywhere from the vacant row homes to shuttered school buildings.

We will discuss solutions as varied as planned shrinkage and programmed immigration. Both solutions address a basic problem that declining cities face. How to continue to provide services to a needy population with a declining tax base? Cities can either creatively decrease the services they provide (planned shrinkage), or they can creatively increase their tax base through growing their population (programmed immigration).

So why are the problems of declining American cities important? According to the 2010 census, one in six Americans – more than 50 million people – live in the 100 largest American cities. According to our definition of a declining city which is a city which has lost population for 3 out of 4 census studies, more than 13 million people, or almost 5% of America's population, live in declining cities. This number surely increases if we expand our scope to include the top 200 or top 500 largest American cities. In these areas, American citizens are retarded in their efforts to live the American dream due to the dysfunctional status of these cities. If we can bail out our leading financial institutions because it is in our national interest, can't we find a way to "bail out" these declining American cities and directly affect the lives of 13 million Americans for the better?

As an urban planner, an affordable housing developer, and native of an American Inner City, I humbly offer this book to President Trump and the Trump Administration as a manifesto which describes new policies for addressing an old problem... how to solve the ails of America's declining cities.

# CHAPTER I

# HOW DID WE GET HERE?

## A.

**S**tates and municipalities around the country are grappling with gaping budget deficits and no easy way to fix it. The Great Recession has forced states and cities to rethink their service delivery models to its citizens. Although only a handful of municipalities have filed bankruptcy because they are unable to meet their obligations, many more municipalities around the country have been forced to cut funding to essential programs or services such as police and health care in order to avoid bankruptcy. This problem has only been exacerbated with the anemic economic growth that has followed the end of the Great Recession of 2008.

Budget deficits and elimination of essential services are more acutely felt in America's oldest urban centers. Many economists, including several from the Brookings Institute, have argued that old American cities have been in decline for decades. The following statistics are so well known in urban policy circles that they do not even require a footnote. Detroit, for example, has lost nearly half its population since 1950. Baltimore, with a population of nearly one million in 1950, now has a population of around 600,000. Youngstown, Ohio, an old steel-manufacturing city, has lost more than half its population, too; while Flint, Michigan, the home of GM and the worst public health crisis in decades, has fared worse. It has lost more than 60% of its population.

Many older American cities have struggled with the downward spiral of a diminished economic base, which leads to a diminished population which, in turn, leads to a diminished tax base. Detroit was a city of nearly two million people but it now has 900,000. The New York Times reported former Mayor David Bing, of Detroit as saying, "We've got to be the best 900,000 populated city we can be and stop thinking about 'We can turn the clock to the 1950s and 60s'. That era is gone." Previous Detroit administrations have discussed ways to bring industry and people back to the city. Mayor Bing is probably the first mayor of a declining major American city to acknowledge that his city is in permanent decline.

Declining cities differ from other cities because of the pervasiveness of this downward spiral of a diminishing economic base leading to a diminished population leading to a further diminished economic base. Whereas other cities may gain or lose industries and populations depending on the phase of the economic cycle, declining cities seem to permanently suffer from a diminishing economic base and diminishing population. Let's explore this further. Below is an example of how this downward spiral begins in our typical, older, declining American city. We'll name our hypothetical city Urbana and place the city in Michigan.

Urbana is a small city with roughly 150,000 residents. It has a rich industrial history and was about 25% larger in its heyday. Urbana, like many industrial towns in the Midwest, supported the auto manufacturing industry and was home to several auto part manufacturers.

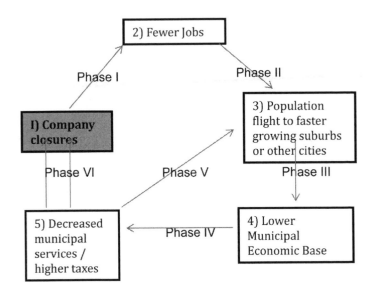

Let's quickly illustrate an example of how this cycle becomes reinforcing.

Phase I: Company Closure – American Car-Parts Manufacturer Entity, or ACME, which sells auto parts to various car manufacturers, has decided to move its factory to Mexico and move the executive offices to Charlotte, North Carolina. The company has its headquarters and a factory in Urbana but has decided to close both. The executive offices were moved to Charlotte to take advantage of the warmer weather and to be closer to large debt and equity investors who primarily have their main offices in Charlotte. The loss of the company's headquarters and manufacturing facility directly leads to job losses.

Phase II: Loss of Jobs – ACME employed 100 people on the factory floor and 15 people in the executive office. Ten executives make the move to Charlotte. All factory workers are laid off except for supervisors who will oversee the contractors in Mexico who make the widgets. Urbana is a small city with approximately 50,000 working adults. The loss of nearly 100 jobs represents a significant loss to this city.

Phase III: Flight to suburbs or faster growing cities – The former employees of the factory are confronted with one of the toughest labor markets in Michigan and highest unemployment rates in the country. Former employees leave the area for job opportunities with similar factories in the Southeast or Texas. Several older employees retire. Only 20 former employees ultimately find jobs in Urbana.

Other employees identify service jobs in the fast growing suburbs around their city. These employees, who are already forced to work in the suburbs, learn first-hand of the better school system, better public safety, and better public health care system and slowly decide to move closer to their new job in the suburbs.

Phase IV: Lower Municipal Tax Base – The loss of the company and 80 jobs represent a loss of 2% of the tax base for Urbana. In a municipality with multiple industries, this loss could be compensated by the growth of another company or another industry. However, the towns and cities in Michigan have primarily been industrial-based economies. Although Detroit is the largest example of a one industry city in Michigan, many cities and towns in Michigan have an economic base that mimicked this model.

Phase V: Increased taxes or lower services – The municipality is confronted with the tough choice of increasing taxes or lowering services to balance its budgets. Remember, cities, unlike the federal government, must balance their budgets every year. Property taxes, once a reliable and growing source of income for this municipality, have decreased because property values have decreased and taxes are based on property values. The loss of the ACME Corporation in Urbana cannot be balanced by an increased property tax base or other growing companies. Increasing taxes will allow the city to keep its current level of services but it will raise taxes on a community already struggling with high unemployment rates. Lowering services will only frustrate the citizens who do not understand why the city can't do a better job with public safety, schools, or sanitation.

Either choice will not only weigh on the employees who were laid-off from this factory, but it will also weigh on the entire community. Residents who were not impacted by the closing of ACME will be affected by the higher taxes or decreased services. Some residents will decide to leave the municipality altogether because it is generally uncompetitive with the surrounding suburbs or other cities that are growing faster.

To understand the downward spiral that declining cities face, Phase V is the critical element. Phases I-IV were the result of one company's closure and the impact on its employees. Phase V impacts all residents of the municipality because the decrease in services and/or the increase in tax rates will make this municipality less competitive compared to neighboring municipalities which may not have experienced such a dramatic flight of industry.

If this cycle does not reverse itself, Urbana, over time, will become a city known for high taxes, diminished public services, or both.

The very nature of the city itself can also change. Urbana may become known as an area where crime is not as heavily enforced as the surrounding suburbs or where the school system is weakening.

The loss of companies, when balanced with the creation of new companies and jobs, is the ideal capitalistic model and indeed works in many cities. Many American cities continue to grow and thrive even when one company shuts down because it can absorb laid-off employees within other companies that are growing and thriving. The loss of the manufacturing base in New York City between the 1950's and 1980's was easily accounted for by the advent of the financial service industries in the 1980's and new media industries during the turn of the century.

When companies begin to leave an area and other industries do not take their place with new jobs, a downward spiral begins to reinforce itself with every loop – a decreased economic base leads to a decreased population which leads a further, steeper decrease in the economic base and population. Phase V, the loss of municipal services or increased taxes, can itself cause even *further* population decline. The decrease in population will only continue to diminish the tax base of a municipality and force it to continue to raise taxes or cut services.

In addition, the downward spiral begins to reinforce itself even before it is completed. Phase V can ultimately lead to Phase VI but can and does lead back to Phase III, which is more population loss.

Phase VI: Additional Company Closures

CEO's of other corporations are also members of Urbana. The options of raising taxes or lowering services are both bad options. Raised taxes will only make an already tough economic environment harder because taxes squeeze profit margins. Lowering municipal services will make it harder to attract good employees who would prefer to live and maybe work somewhere besides Urbana. As residents leave because of the municipality's decision to cut services or raise taxes, CEO's of other corporations will begin to question if this is a good place for them to do business. Some will decide to leave for a place with a higher concentration of customers.

Additional company closures are analogous to dominoes falling. The first domino to fall is a willful act. The other dominoes are a by-product of the first.

Cities have tried to counter this by increasing the tax rate on remaining residents and businesses. Unfortunately, businesses have become more mobile. And better educated and/or higher income households are also fairly mobile and attracted to suburban communities for a host of reasons. David Rusk in "A Strategy for Regional Renewal" described how these factors have impacted Baltimore, a declining American city. Increased tax rates only provide another incentive for these stakeholders to leave the urban center for suburbs or more vibrant cities. Consequently, increased tax rates lead to a further diminished economic base which gets the downward spiral going.

*tax rates*

The spiral can be broken through the creation of new industries or the growth of companies in existing industries. However, many Midwestern and Northeastern cities were heavily dependent on manufacturing. Companies in high growth industries such as finance, technology or energy have little incentive to locate to these declining cities.

Unable to break this cycle, many older, American cities have become home to those households which are least mobile and poor. Unable to raise the tax rate any further, older American cities have been forced to cut essential services. These essential services include public education, public safety performed by police and firemen, and public health which is usually performed by the public hospitals. The decrease in these essential services creates a further incentive for the remaining middle class in these cities to leave, and it further depresses the quality of life of poor residents who are unable to leave.

This downward spiral is a slow death sentence for a city and its remaining residents. Why would anyone stay in a city with declining services and higher taxes? Cities have blamed their misfortune on the improving fortunes of surrounding suburbs. It is true that surrounding suburbs of older declining cities have better schools and better health care options. They also tend to have a lower tax base. This is achievable since the citizens of these suburbs produce more income than the average citizen in a declining city and these areas have more vibrant commercial activity on a per capita basis. However, this trend of urban residents leaving older cities for the suburbs or more vibrant, newer cities becomes a spiral because it feeds on itself.

Ultimately, the remaining residents of a declining city become the least mobile and employable in the metropolitan area. Although cities continue to attract young college graduates looking for a cooler lifestyle, these individuals will inevitably leave the city once they have children or begin to understand the true meaning of high taxes.

If you have looked at the news in the past 30 years or have parents or grandparents that lived in a declining city, you have probably noticed this trend for yourself. Older people talk whimsically about the good ole' days when everyone in their neighborhood was striving to do better. They may also discuss how their neighborhood was much more vibrant when they grew up. Schools seemed to function better. Streets were cleaner. Residents, even though they may have been poor, were optimistic and proud.

Besides population loss, declining cities tend to follow several common trends. They are predominately located in the colder climates of the Northeast and Midwest. Their economic base was once dominated by a single industry that has sharply declined since World War II. And they have been unable to attract growth industries that could create jobs and opportunities to advance business growth. Successive administrations in these cities have tried, to no avail, to raise taxes in order to continue the delivery of basic services to its citizens. As more middle class residents flee, this strategy no longer works, and administrations are forced to cut services.

Baltimore is a classic example. Many academics and politicians, including David Rusk who is the former mayor of Albuquerque, have written extensively about the decline of this city. I'll highlight the story of a dilapidated commercial corridor in Baltimore later in this chapter. However, there are many dilapidated corridors and dilapidated residential neighborhoods in Baltimore. "The Wire," a critically acclaimed television series on HBO about an inner city neighborhood in Baltimore, highlights the struggles the police face in trying to stop a pervasive culture of drugs and crime in a neighborhood in West Baltimore. "The Wire" showed the rest of the country what many Baltimoreans have known for a while. Baltimore is on the decline.

Baltimore's history is typical of a declining city. It was dominated by strong activity from its ports and manufacturing base. The city grew quickly between 1880 and World War II. It attracted European immigrants and African-Americans from the South to work in its docks and factories. During this 60-year period, the population more than doubled. After World War II, the manufacturing base fled the city. Its port was overtaken by larger ports on the Eastern seaboard. The

White middle class fled in the 1960's and the Black middle class followed in the 1970's and 1980's. Baltimore, a city that once approached one million people, now has a population of approximately 600,000.

The leaders of Baltimore during the 1910's tried to plan for the growth of the city by incorporating suburbs and building an infrastructure to support one million residents. Like any good municipal administrator, the leaders of the city understood that infrastructure improvements take time. They built roads, sewer lines, and schools to ensure that the city's infrastructure did not hamper the growth of the city. It is this same infrastructure which accounts for so many of the dilapidated structures found in Baltimore today.

In 2005, my partner and I began a small real estate development company in Baltimore to take advantage of the credit bubble and rows of empty townhomes. We were both from New York City and were attracted to the lack of competition for properties in Baltimore compared to the Big Apple. My partner moved to Baltimore while I commuted from New York weekly.

While visiting Baltimore for a business meeting, my partner took me to a corner in a blighted but potentially up and coming neighborhood. We stood on the corner for 30 minutes next to a development opportunity. We talked for a while and then he asked me if I noticed anything missing.

After several minutes of playing his guessing game, I gave up and asked for the answer. His response was simple. We hadn't seen any presence of police. We did not see a police car or patrol during the entire time.

As veterans of inner city real estate development in inner city neighborhoods, we acutely understood the importance of safety to a community. By 2007, Baltimore had much worse crime statistics than New York City. Baltimore was also smaller and arguably easier to patrol. However, the police presence in Baltimore was scant. The neighborhood that we were interested in did indeed have many strong attributes, which should have created high demand for its apartments and houses. It was adjacent to a beautiful park, it was less than 15 minutes from downtown, and the neighborhood was filled with vacant or dilapidated historic homes with great architecture. Although my partner and I had seen many neighborhoods like this in New York City become transformed, this neighborhood in Baltimore is *still* filled with many run-down, empty buildings. There are probably lots of reasons why this is the case but a major one is the city's inability to provide public safety.

Although most cities benefitted from the recent economic bubble during the latter half of the last decade, it is obvious now that the bubble was not sustainable. Younger adults were drawn to the vibrant urban core and entertainment options only found in cities. Although this trend was more pronounced in places like New York, Chicago, and Los Angeles that benefitted from globalized job creation, older American cities at least experienced a temporary reprieve from decades of population decline and diminishing economic opportunities. The Great Recession surely eliminated this trend and the anemic growth which followed in this decade hasn't helped. The divergent outcomes of successful versus declining cities will be discussed later in this book.

Several economists recently spotlighted by CBS News have predicted that this recession will be followed by stagnant long-term growth similar to the 1970's. The recession of the 1970's commenced with bloated budget deficits from the Vietnam War and a severe energy crisis that created fuel shortages. The decade was then marked with stagnant growth and increasing inflation. Although the recession of the early 1970's ended in 1974, the recovery of jobs, wealth and income did not occur until almost ten years later in 1983. Just imagine the painful cuts being made across the country lasting for the remainder of this decade. How will older American cities adjust to another seven years of diminishing population and a diminishing economic base?

## B.

Today, declining cities are littered with vacant houses and abandoned commercial centers because the populations have fled. Mayors of these cities mistakenly try to address this problem by using limited municipal resources to perform a cosmetic fix to a particular neighborhood. Theneighborhood is usually chosen because of some historical significance or important landmark.

Let's return to Baltimore.

The Pennsylvania Avenue Redevelopment Collaborative (PARC) was established in 2000 to promote the cultural and economic redevelopment of the most prominent African-American neighborhood in Baltimore, the Pennsylvania Avenue corridor, or "the Avenue." Like the Harlem Renaissance during the 1920's, it was home to a significant African-American cultural revolution and had several cultural venues, including the Royal Theater and the Regent. Although the Apollo Theatre in Harlem is better known, the Regent was also home to many African-American jazz and theatrical performers.

Ninety year-old Northwest Baltimore resident Clarence "Shad" Brown still takes an occasional trip down memory lane to remember the Avenue during its heyday. Health reasons prevent him from actually making the drive a few miles south to the street itself, but sitting at his dining room table, dressed comfortably in a striped T-shirt and gray sweatpants, he's only too happy to take a mental trip back to the days when he might find himself standing on the Avenue on a warm sunny day wearing a stylish, three-piece suit. In fact, he says, you wouldn't be caught dead there wearing anything but your finest and sharpest threads.

> "Yeah, the Avenue was the spot," Brown beams with pride. "I can name every store, club, and every bar all the way up [the street]."

Brown describes Pennsylvania Avenue from what was called "the bottom," near where he lived on Hoffman Street, up to North Avenue, stopping at places like the Club Casino, Ike Dixon's Comedy Club, Gamby's, and the Sphinx Club. Brown recalls he mingled with a stream of ordinary people— from laborers to doctors and teachers—all dressed to the nines in hats, dresses, gloves, furs, suits, and zoot suits. Like Brown, they were often heading to the Royal or Regent theaters, or one of the innumerable bars and nightclubs lining the street. And at the Royal Theater, patrons could pay 50 to 75 cents ($1 for the midnight show) to see the likes of Cab Calloway, Dizzy Gillespie, Duke Ellington, Billie Holiday, and Dinah Washington at the nearly 1,400-seat luxury theater, and then catch a glimpse of the same stars later at famed hot spots like the Avenue Bar or the Alhambra Grill.

> "I get tired of people talking about the Harlem Renaissance, because Baltimore had a renaissance, too," Phillip Merrill says.

Phillip J. Merrill, a Baltimore native, is a collector, historian, author, and appraiser for PBS's *Antiques Roadshow*. He specializes in African-American history, specifically the physical relics of black culture. Through his firm, Nanny Jack and Co., Merrill consults on exhibits, tours, and seminars, brokers black memorabilia, rents artifacts to film companies, and provides stock photography rentals and research. His work encompasses African-American history as a whole, but he has a special interest in his hometown.

There were so many African-American Baltimoreans thriving on and around Pennsylvania Avenue during the early and mid-20th century that all you had to do for a list was, well, pick up a directory. That's exactly what Merrill has, pulling out *The First Colored Professional, Clerical and Business Directory of Baltimore City*, a small, weathered blue booklet printed with block letters, first published in 1913 by an African-American man named Robert Coleman. Coleman continued to publish directories annually until his death in 1946.

Although the directories were published years before Merrill was born, they are clearly his babies; he allows a reporter to leaf through a laminated ninth edition, published in 1921 and featuring a portrait of Coleman inside, but the 1913 first edition is off limits. "It's too fragile," he explains.

It is easy to understand why Merrill is so zealous about these modest booklets. They provide a front-row seat to the lives that ordinary residents of the Pennsylvania Avenue area lived back then. About 60 years after the Emancipation Proclamation, the 1921-22 edition of Coleman's directory lists 21 black dentists, nine of whose practices were on the Avenue. The name of African-American attorney George W.F. McMechen leaps from one page; as Morgan College's – now Morgan State University's – first graduate in 1895, McMechen has a building at the school named in his honor.

The directory also includes listings for two mine operators, 12 notaries public, seven nurses, 44 physicians, and 28 organizations, including the Arch Social Club, the Colored High School Alumni Association, the Du Bois Circle (named for W.E.B. Du Bois), the Inter-Racial Conference, the Maryland Association for the Colored Blind, the Maryland Colored Public Health Association, the NAACP, and the Marcus Garvey-led black nationalist group, the Universal Negro Improvement Association, which once had an office at 1917 Pennsylvania Avenue.

Given the historical nature of the Avenue, the support that PARC has received from neighborhood residents and the city is understandable. The city has given nearly $1,000,000 toward the redevelopment of the Avenue. However, the best efforts of the city and local residents cannot reverse what the city of Baltimore has experienced since the 1960's. Baltimore has lost more than one-third of its population. And right now, it ranks as one of the most dangerous big cities in the country.

Pennsylvania Avenue has not been spared. All of the theatres that made it the African-American cultural mecca of Baltimore have shuddered. The Avenue is now known more for narcotics sales and vacant buildings. A police shooting highlights the despair that residents in this neighborhood are subjected to. Dante Arthur, an undercover police officer, was shot and wounded while making an undercover drug buy in a housing development near Pennsylvania Avenue in 2009. Although the city immediately held several community meetings after the incident, residents were frustrated that it took a police shooting for the city to pay attention to rampant drug activity.

Said a woman from the neighborhood during a community meeting, "The police patrols have really gone down, and since then, the drug activity has really escalated. I can tell you exactly what the dealers look like. I know who they are. They look right into my eyes. People sit in their cars in front of my house and smoke marijuana. I talk to them. They talk to me.

I'm pretty bold and I don't care. I want them to know that I'm watching them."

Another woman stated: "We're stuck here. We can't go out and we can't get in. We can't go outside. When we hear gunshots, we hit the floor. When we call the police, they come to our house and then everyone knows we called. You know we don't call the police because we live in fear every day."

If a local resident realizes the rampant crime and drug activity in this neighborhood, surely the leaders of city government also understand the problem. However, the problems discussed by the women who attended this community meeting are not isolated to the Pennsylvania Avenue corridor. They are repeated throughout many parts of the city. Baltimore simply does not have the resources to address the crime in its many distressed neighborhoods. The story of the Avenue is repeated over and over in many formerly vibrant commercial corridors throughout America's older cities.

Imagine living through the conditions described by these women at this community meeting in Baltimore. Gunshots are horrifying. They are horrifying when soldiers hear them in combat, and they are especially horrifying near your house when you are trying to raise a family. However, these women are complaining about a symptom, not a problem. The gunshots are not the problem. The poor drug dealing teenagers who are shooting the guns that create the gunshots are not the problem. Every city has poor drug-dealing teenagers. A city's inability to effectively address this problem due to budget deficits and lack of public safety resources is the *real* problem.

Unfortunately, this neighborhood meeting even if it involved the police chief from the local precinct, was bound to be fruitless. In a declining city like Baltimore, public safety resources like police are stretched thin. The police chief, even if he wanted to, could not convince the mayor to increase the police presence throughout the entire city because the city is already on a tight budget.

Even if the residents of this neighborhood are effective in gathering a greater police presence later on, it will simply mean that another neighborhood in Baltimore will have a lowered police presence. Neighborhood meetings, even when successful, only move the problem to another neighborhood that will have its own meeting about a drug related crime incidednt a few months or a year down the line.

C.

*he Fiscal Cliff* is not another diatribe about the dire straits of residents living in failing American cities. The literature on these two subjects is extensive and exhaustive enough. If you are reading this book, you probably have a sensitivity, interest, or passion in the problems that impact the residents of failing American cities and have yourself read a few of these books already. As you can imagine, I have also read quite a few of them myself. And the problems described there, and described even more vividly by the women of the Pennsylvania Avenue corridor in Baltimore, have indeed proven stubborn. But stubborn problems require equally forceful solutions.

This book will illustrate how real change for our failing cities can only occur through structural, not marginal change. Mayors of American cities intimately understand the definition of a Catch-22. State guidelines mandate that cities must have balanced budgets annually. Cities and states, unlike the federal government, cannot run annual deficits. Diminished tax revenue due to lower property taxes, income taxes, and sales taxes from the Great Recession has forced mayors to cut municipal budgets. However, the Great Recession has also put more demands on municipalities because more residents are unemployed but still in need of food, health care, and housing.

As a developer of residential housing in New York City during the 1990's and 2000's, I've seen firsthand how quickly neighborhoods can change under the right circumstances. New York reached a low point in the early 1990's. The recession of the early 1990's decimated an already diminished manufacturing base in the city. Population had declined significantly. The city that today has more than 8,000,000 people only had 7,000,000 people in 1990. Formerly vibrant commercial corridors such as 125th Street in Harlem and Fulton Avenue in Brooklyn were barren. The city was giving away excess homes.

By the mid-1990's, several things occurred to fuel New York City's current growth. Crime began a sharp decline and became a major focus for the mayoral administration. Fast growing global industries such as finance and media took the place of manufacturing.

The jobs created by these and other industries were filled by an immigration boom. In fact, more immigrants came to New York during this time than any other, including the famous immigration boom during the early 1900's. Although many families today can trace their lineage to Ellis Island, going forward, even more families will be able to trace their lineage to Kennedy Airport, the Canadian border or any other of the various entry points their family used to enter New York City during the 1990's.

Today, New York City has more people than ever. It is again a shining example of a fast growing and wealthy American city. Crime is at its lowest point in nearly 50 years. In the same neighborhoods that I began my development career renovating dilapidated rental buildings, condominiums easily sell for $1,000,000. These changes did not occur overnight. They are due to significant structural changes that occurred nearly two decades prior.

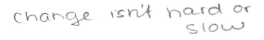

change isn't hard or slow

## D.

Through real, structural changes, municipal leaders and their citizens can experience growth and prosperity even in declining cities. These changes will take time. But they *will* yield results. I've seen it! *The Fiscal Cliff* will explore a few possible solutions for declining American cities and ways to implement those changes.

But before discussing possible solutions, let's gain a better understanding of the true problem that declining cities face.

The promulgation of large-scale cities is a relatively recent phenomenon. During the height of the British Empire, London was the largest city in the world. In 1801, London had more than 1,000,000 people. By the end of the 19th century, London's population was in excess of 3,000,000. In 1800, no other city in the world had 1,000,000 people. Before London in 1800, the only other city with more than 1,000,000 people was ancient Rome.

People had little reason to live in cities in the 19th century or before. They were dirty and crowded. The rural life was hard but provided a clean and healthy lifestyle. Even today, many urban dwellers will pay a great deal of money to have vacations in rural or tropical environments. Many niches of the vacation industry, in fact, cater to urban dwellers who want to be closer to nature.

Thomas Jefferson, one of our founding fathers and the third President of the United States, argued against the growth of cities for the United States. He saw cities as breeding grounds for moral decay and poor public health. He advocated strongly for a country based on an agrarian lifestyle. Probably his most significant accomplishment, the creation of the University of Virginia, is a testimony to his belief that an open, natural environment is best for a society. The University of Virginia is a great college campus known for its lush green scenery and beautiful landscape. It is also several hours from the busy cities in the Mid-Atlantic corridor.

London's explosive growth during the 18th and 19th century can be primarily explained through the advent of the Industrial Revolution and its strategic important as the main trading hub for the British Empire. During the 17th and 18th century, people from all over the British Isles came to London to experience the increased economic opportunities offered in the city. In short, London was a dynamic economic engine that created jobs for people tired of the brutal existence offered by a rural lifestyle.

Today, there are 150 cities in the world with more than 1,000,000 people. The formation of these cities and the rationale for their growth is the same as it was for London nearly

200 years ago. These cities are <u>hubs of industry and trade</u>. People continue to come to these cities to seek <u>increased economic opportunities</u>. Whether it's rural farmers in China who seek factory jobs in China's coastal cities, or rural Mexicans searching for jobs in the cities of the United States, people come to cities for jobs.

This urbanization of America coincided with the second industrial age. The Second Industrial Revolution (1880-1910), which began after the America Civil War and the advent of the railways, turned America's Northeastern and Midwestern cities into economic hubs for their entire metropolitan area. Before the Second Industrial Revolution, America was primarily a rural country. Cities existed but were mainly home to merchants, bars, and seats of government. Most people went to these cities to trade goods and return to their farms.

The Second Industrial Revolution also saw the advent of large and small manufacturers who took advantage of new industrial technologies to mass produce goods. New Haven, Connecticut was known for its gun manufacturing. Flint, Michigan was the original home of General Motors. New York's garment industry supplied the United States and parts of Western Europe with clothes. As people clamored to get these jobs, cities in the Northeast and Midwest experienced explosive growth.

There are several reasons why cities in the Northeast and Midwest experienced significant population and economic growth during this period compared to other parts of the county. After the Civil War, the Midwest and Northeast were the most developed parts of the country. The Civil War had decimated the South. The South was primarily a rural culture and needed slavery to maintain its predominant way of life. Few cities in the South were positioned to benefit from the Second Industrial Revolution even before the war. The infrastructure in these cities that could have supported the Industrial Revolution was destroyed during the war.

As for the West, it was still being incorporated into the United States during this period. Most of our western states were still a state of Mexico until the Mexican-American War of the 1830's. Moreover, the United States' continuing battle to eradicate its Native American population and claim their territories was still occurring during the late 19th century in the Northwest. Have you ever wondered where Seattle, the leading city in the Northwest, got its name? Chief Seattle was the last Native American chief who claimed sovereignty over the area near the Puget Sound. He was killed in 1866. Washington State did not even become a state of the United States until 1890.

The Northeast and Midwest, in contrast, comprised the original 13 states and the oldest states thereafter. These territories already had an existing infrastructure and established transportation modes. The Erie Canal, which spurred the initial growth of New York City in the 18th century, was built well before the Second Industrial Revolution. The Northeast and Midwest also had a well-built railroad system which was lacking in the Deep South and rural West. The old B & O (Baltimore & Ohio) railroad was instrumental in transporting raw goods from America's hinterlands into Baltimore. These raw goods were then manufactured into finished goods and shipped to Western Europe for consumption.

Manufacturing countries need to export their goods to countries that have a demand for them. China's current explosive growth is greatly assisted by the strong demand for their goods in Western Europe, Japan, and the United States. The largest trading partner for the United States at the start of the Second Industrial Revolution was Western Europe. The cities in the Northeast, with their proximity to Europe, were best positioned to absorb this demand for goods and raw material from Europe. Port cities in the Northeast and Mid-Atlantic, such as New York, Boston, and Baltimore, became major trading hubs. Cities in the Midwest, such as St. Louis and Kansas City, near river and railroad access also became hubs for the transportation of raw and finished goods.

Between 1880 and 1920, these cities experienced explosive growth. The population of Baltimore doubled from 330,000 to 700,000. The population of Cleveland more than quadrupled from 160,000 to 700,000, while the population of Newark, New Jersey tripled from 135,000 to 410,000. Pick any major Midwestern or Northeastern city, and they all exhibited tremendous growth during this 40-year period. Immigrants from Europe and African-Americans from the American South flooded these cities looking for opportunities. Although cities also offered recreational and cultural opportunities for residents, the unprecedented growth of these cities during the Second Industrial Revolution proves that the primary driver for the growth of American cities was and continues to be economic opportunity.

After World War II, the advent of highways and the transportation of goods by trucks instead of rail or ship allowed manufacturing firms to relocate away from the dense cities of the Northeast and Midwest and to move to the more expansive and warmer areas of the South and West. Globalization and the ease of trade and communication across the globe has further allowed firms to move facilities away from the expensive labor markets of the United States and to cheaper labor markets in Asia and Latin America. The rise of Globalization since World War II and especially since the 1980's has been a primary factor in the de-industrialization of America and the consequential de-population of many cities, mostly in the Midwest and Northeast, that relied on manufacturing as their main industry.

Unfortunately, the United States simply does not need as many manufacturing or trading hubs in a global economy. The urbanization model which worked for the United States during the first half of the 20th century does not work in a global economy of the 21$^{st}$ century. As the United States shifts from a manufacturing economy to a service economy – which exports financial services, media, Internet, and technology instead of cars, clothes, and other simple goods – fewer hubs are needed to export these goods. Moreover, these hubs can now be located in warmer climates that do not need to be located near railway hubs or rivers. These developments do not bode well for the older industrial cities in the Northeast and Midwest. And there is no identifiable replacement for the jobs which manufacturing provided to these cities.

The United States is not unique in this regard. There have been extensive studies on declining cities by the London School of Economics. The London School of Economics (LSE) recently completed a study of seven older, industrial European cities. The purpose of the LSE study was to chronicle the decline of these cities and study the various ways that these cities have attempted to revitalize. Similar to their American counterparts, these cities were located near natural resources such as coal, and they became major trading and manufacturing hubs for their regional area.

Declining cities, just like vibrant cities, are not aberrations. Many planners and municipal administrators mistakenly view cities as static entities. I argue that cities need to be viewed as fluid entities that can experience both growth and decline. The history of cities proves this to be true. In the extreme examples, adventurous travelers pay a great deal of money to view the ruins of ancient cities. Some ancient cities were leveled by war. Others were just abandoned.

Central America is littered with ancient Mayan settlements. These settlements, which predate the discovery of Columbus by hundreds of years, housed great Mayan buildings and were trading hubs for the Mayan empire. Historians still debate why the Mayans abandoned these cities. Some claim that a major drought caused the abandonment while others claim that disease or an unknown war leveled the population. Although the root cause is in question, the fact remains that these great cities were indeed abandoned.

All cities experience great growth periods followed by periods of stabilization and decline. As we discussed earlier, most people prefer the tranquility, safety, and healthy aspects of nature compared to the cramp conditions of a city. Cities need a reason to exist. That reason is primarily jobs. When jobs leave, people leave with them.

If we stop viewing cities as static entities and recognized the dynamism that is at the very core of all cities, the growth and eventual decline of a city would seem obvious If we compare cities to living creatures, jobs would be the nourishment that feeds all other aspects of the body. Although the cultural aspects or architectural aspects of a city are celebrated, they become irrelevant without jobs to support its residents. In much the same way, a person with a great mind or amazing muscular capabilities becomes feeble without proper nour-ishment to feed them.

What happens to a city when the jobs no longer exist? What happens when the jobs leave forever? Can cities plan for their eventual decline?

CHAPTER II

# WHAT IS A DECLINING CITY?

A.

**A**s an adult, I've had the privilege of driving cross-county… twice. The United States is a large country with a rich diversity of architectural styles and urban plans. During my first trip in 1999, I drove south from New York City to New Orleans, and then proceeded west to Las Vegas. My second trip in 2002 took me west from New York City through the Midwest and Rocky Mountain Regions to Seattle. Both trips were great learning experiences. As a native New Yorker, the scenic beauty of the Southwest region in cities such as Santa Fe was striking. The newness of cities in the West was also surprising. Seattle was only incorporated in 1865 while the recent growth of Las Vegas from a casino-centric town to a thriving city has meant the replacement of desert with new housing subdivisions. The United States of America is indeed a beautiful country.

Driving cross-country also allowed me to see the differences in American cities by region. Ever wonder why New York is so dense while Los Angeles barely has a downtown district? Ever wonder why Detroit has massive boulevards throughout the city while some streets in Boston or Baltimore can barely fit two cars side by side? These differences result from the variables that caused the birth and growth of particular cities. Most cities in the Northeast achieved their initial growth before the advent of the automobile. In the 19th century, most workers walked to work, and horses were the primary mode of transportation. Only the wealthy had the time and access to speedy transportation to make living beyond walking distance to their jobs a possibility. The need for close proximity to work resulted in the density of America's earlier cities.

Automobiles allowed cities in the West and South to be more decentralized. By observing cities as diverse as Cleveland, Ohio; Kansas City, MO; Lubbock, TX; and Seattle, WA with my own eyes, I could better understand why and how these cities were created in the first place.

My trips cross-country, in fact spurred me to write this book. It's one thing to theoretically understand that certain cities do and do not work. It is entirely something else to see it firsthand. Moreover, observations gave me better insight on why these cities were created in the first place. By understanding that cities are indeed created and do indeed grow, it helped me understand that cities can also decline if the rational for its continuation is not persuasive.

I also spent time in as many working-class communities across the country as possible. I was curious to know how the development of these communities mimicked the neighborhood of my youth in New York City. Although poor and working-class neighborhoods had unfortunate similarities throughout the country, it was not monolithic. Cities in the Northeast and Midwest, such as Detroit and Kansas City, had decaying infrastructure with large and vacant office buildings in the urban core. The surrounding residential neighborhoods were underutilized and had a substantial number of abandoned housing structures or unoccupied land.

Observing and learning about the history of the arch in St. Louis was insightful. The arch represented America's expansion westward during the 19th century. Seeing the complete abandonment of East St. Louis and the other inner city neighborhoods around St. Louis was also insightful – but for a different reason. These older Midwestern cities had an infrastructure – housing, schools, and office buildings – that was relevant in a previous era but now clearly existed in service to no one.

The cities I observed in the West also had working class communities. However, when I observed working class communities in Denver, Seattle or Las Vegas, the infrastructure was neither old nor underutilized.   Although there were disparities between homes in downtown Denver and Martin Luther King Boulevard in Denver, (I hope the reference to MLK Boulevard is not lost to you. Chris Rock said if you ever want to find a depressed neighborhood in any city just find Martin Luther King Boulevard.) the housing stock along Martin Luther King Boulevard was occupied and the commercial corridor was not abandoned.

The Western States and Rocky Mountain states were developed and grew primarily after America's industrial revolution. The Infrastructure of these cities were not predicated on growth assumptions created in the 19th century but on more recent assumptions based on more modern industries. Abandonment does exist in these Western cities but not on the scale of the cities in the Midwest or Northeast. This is primarily due to the elimination of the main growth engine for many cities in the Midwest and Northeast..... the manufacturing industry.

## B.

**N**ew Haven, Connecticut is the home Yale University. Yale annually ranks as one of the top five universities in the country; it has the second largest endowment in the country (Harvard is first); and was formed before the founding of our country. To mention Yale as an elite college is an understatement. Three of our last five presidents have attended Yale University as an undergraduate or law student. Yale students are not only leaders in politics but also in businesses and media.

Yale also is the largest employer in New Haven. This was not always the case. New Haven was once a vibrant manufacturing and port city. Eli Whitney is best known as the inventor of the cotton gin machine, which transformed agricultural life in the antebellum South. He was also the owner of a gun manufacturing company in New Haven. By World War II, his company had become the Winchester Arms Company and was the largest employer in New Haven. New Haven was also known as a leading manufacturer of clocks and carriages in the 19th and early parts of the 20th century. The population of the city swelled to 164,000 by 1950.

Immigrants from Europe, and later African-American immigrants from the South, transformed New Haven during the early and mid-parts of the 20th century. The city's growing manufacturing base easily absorbed these new immigrants.

Today, nearly one in four New Haven families live below the poverty line. The next largest employer beside Yale University is the Yale-New Haven Hospital system. Both employers are non-profits and do not add to the city's tax base. Once vibrant neighborhoods, such as Dixwell, Dwight, and Newhallville, are now home to empty houses and high crime rates. After reaching its peak population in the 1950's, the population has declined by nearly 30%.

The results of New Haven's attempts to spur economic activity since the 1960's until now have been decidedly mixed. The demolition of the New Haven Coliseum in 2007 is symptomatic of those efforts. These efforts were highlighted a few years ago by Jonathan Finer of the Washington Post. The coliseum, also known as Veteran's Memorial Coliseum, was constructed in 1972. The coliseum, through increased pedestrian and vehicular traffic, was designed to generate increased economic activity for the surrounding neighborhood. However, at a condemnation hearing in 2003, Mayor Destafano admitted that the town couldn't even sustain a bar on the same block. The Coliseum never created the type of economic activity or pedestrian traffic envisioned by its creators.

The decline of the manufacturing base of New Haven does not have an easy solution. Although the correlation between the diminished manufacturing base and the decreasing residential population is obvious, the strategy for reversing the trend is not. For example, the city's attempt to use a stopgap measure such as the construction of the Coliseum proved to be fruitless.

C.

**A**lthough many American cities are declining, many others have grown significantly in the past 20 years. The reasons for growth can generally be divided into three broad categories: globalization, weather, and tourism. These rationales were highlighted by Anthony Downs of the Brookings Institute in his seminal book on urban decline "Urban Decline and the Future of American Cities."

Several large cities have transformed themselves from manufacturing centers to centers of globalism. After losing its manufacturing base in the 1970's, New York City became a global leader not only in finance but also in media and entertainment. Since 1990, New York City has gained nearly 1.5 million new residents. In other words, more people have moved to New York than all the people that reside in the City of Philadelphia. Los Angeles has also experienced steady growth during this time due to its global leadership position in entertainment and trade. The ports around Los Angeles, bolstered by trade from China, are the busiest in the country. While many cities declined or only sustained population between 1980 and 2005, the population of Los Angeles increased by nearly one-third. Another city that has benefitted from globalism is Seattle. Companies such as Microsoft and Boeing have caused significant economic development and population growth there, which has cemented the city as a leader in technology and high-skill manufacturing. Globalism has clearly transformed certain cities for the better.

Other cities have benefitted from their position in warmer climates. The cities in the Southwest and Sunbelt regions of the United States have shown steady growth for nearly two decades. Phoenix, Charlotte, and San Diego are three prime examples. Houston and San Antonio in Texas have also benefitted from warmer climates and the energy industries. Until our most recent recession, Americans have shown a clear preference for cities in warmer climates. I suspect this trend will continue once Americans, en masse, have the means to continue to relocate away from the colder cities of the Northeast and Midwest.

Several cities have benefitted as domestic and international tourist destinations. Miami has developed a legendary reputation as a tourist destination for people from Latin American, the Caribbean, and all around the U.S. Las Vegas has grown due to its reputation as a tourist destination and nightlife. Las Vegas and the surrounding counties have been the fastest growing counties in the country since 1990.

Older cities, specifically in the Midwest, Northeast/ Mid-Atlantic regions, do not benefit from any of the factors mentioned above. These cities have been practically defined by their cold winters. Moreover, their declining manufacturing base has not been replaced by global industries. It's been proven time and time again that successful cities are able to export services or goods domestically and, more importantly, internationally. Think of Miami and tourism or Charlotte and the banking industry. Without weather as a magnet or industries which can benefit from the advent of globalism, Declining cities have few options for advancement.

Chicago, an older American city, has been able to avoid the fate of other cities in the Midwest because of the growth of the financial and media industries. The financial industry in Chicago has grown significantly in the past 10 years. However, Chicago already had a significant financial industry that catered to the many manufacturing and transport companies located in that city. Detroit, unfortunately, never developed such a strong financial service industry. The same is true for Cleveland, Youngstown, Buffalo and many other Midwest and Northeast cities. Although these declining cities could develop new industries like green technology that appeal to the global market, it is doubtful that these industries could grow to a scale that would significantly impact the economic base of these cities. In short, declining cities must acknowledge that their economic base and population have been *permanently affected* by the loss of previous economic drivers such as manufacturing.

The problems that confront declining cities are substantially different than those affecting declining neighborhoods in otherwise healthy or growing cities. All cities have neighborhoods that have above average poverty levels and/or above average unemployment levels. San Francisco, arguably one of the wealthiest cities in the country, has the Tenderloin district. The Tenderloin district is known for its high concentration of homeless shelters and crime. New York City is still home to the South Bronx, which is the poorest county in the country. Chicago still must contend with high poverty and crime rates on the west side of the city.

*The difference between declining cities and declining neighborhoods in otherwise vibrant cities is that declining cities are nearly incapable of dealing with these issues.* New York City can address crime in the city by concentrating police forces in high crime neighborhoods. Chicago can fund creative educational strategies to create public boarding schools and other specialized schools that can better work with challenged students.

Declining cities suffer from all the problems exhibited in declining neighborhoods in vibrant cities but do not have the revenue to address these issues. Many declining cities have suffered from decades of a declining economic base and corresponding declining population. Declining populations lead to vacant properties, declining property values, and declining commercial activity that services a residential population. ***In short, declining cities face a fiscal cliff of unsustainable budgets and increasing demand for services from its residents.***

This downward spiral described in Chapter One, or what I have called unplanned shrinkage, is a structurally different problem than those faced by vibrant cities with bad neighborhoods face. Whereas New York City can argue the benefits of funding charter schools over public schools, Detroit public school system is bankrupt and has a school system controlled by the State.

We have all been witnesses to unplanned shrinkage in many American Cities since the 1960's. No public official could have predict the rapid population declines experienced by many cities in the Midwest and the Northeast. However, the effect of unplanned shrinkage has resulted in the slow declination in the quality of life for Americans living in these cities.

The Flint water crises is simply the latest example of a declining city confronting the realities of unplanned shrinkage. The administration in Flint decided to alter the water delivery service to the city in order to save $5,000,000. Given its persistently declining tax base and need to continue to provide basic services to its residents, saving $5,000,000 was necessary and done with a good intention. We know now that the impact of this decision has been disastrous. We will discuss this further in the book.

Although these older cities have a weakening economic base, they *do* still have a base. Baltimore, with the John

Hopkins University system, Inner Harbor commercial area, the Baltimore Port, and financial service industry, still has an economic base. The first step in addressing unplanned shrinkage is to consider the current and projected economic base of a city. Once the potential economic base is identified, a ratio of economic base to optimal population size can be determined. By comparing the optimal population size to the current population size of a city, planners can define the likelihood of unplanned shrinkage within an urban center. This analysis becomes even more important given the likelihood of unplanned shrinkage in this current economic environment.

## D.

So far, I've made the assertion that declining American cities are a result of a declining economic base. The anecdotal argument for this case is easy to make. Urban planners and journalist often use Detroit as the classic example of how deindustrialization of a city can lead to the depopulation of a city. Indeed, this hypothesis has been argued for decades. Although you have read and will read numerous accounts of how deindustrialization has led to the depopulation of our older cities, a nagging question remains. Is this true? If we look more closely at a representative sample of American cities, can we see a definitive cause and effect between deindustrialization and depopulation? Let's examine the facts.

With the help of several capable research assistants, I analyzed socio-economic data of the largest 100 American cities between 1970 and 2010. Specifically, I analyzed changes in the population size and the changes in economic base of these cities. The economic base was defined as using the number of jobs and adult population in a particular city. The number of jobs was defined by the number of employed people. By dividing the number of jobs or employed people by the adult population, we created our economic base ratio. The analysis is included at the end of this chapter.

Economic Base Ratio = Number of Jobs in a Municipality / Size of Population in Municipality

Economic Base Ratio (EBR) = JOBS / POPULATION

The methodology of our economic base ratio is different than the unemployment ratio typically sited by economists or journalists. The unemployment ratio is simply the number of unemployed adults looking for work divided by the number of all people looking for work. However, the unemployment ratio does not factor in the multitudes of adults who are not looking for employment. This category can include stay-at-home parents rearing their children, older adults who are retired, adults who return to school to continue their education, or any number of people who are not seeking employment.

Our economic base ratio factors in all these people. Ultimately, the economic base of a city is only determined by the number of jobs or the number of employed people in that area. Employed individuals pay taxes, buy goods, and pay for necessary services. Adults who are not employed and not looking for work are a drag to the economic vibrancy of a city. Although unemployed people do not pay taxes, they still demand basic public services such as health care and public safety.

For example, children and seniors are a necessary part of any functioning society but do not contribute as much to the economic vitality of a municipality as do working adults.

Traditional unemployment ratios do not capture any of the activity of adults who are not actively looking for work. A city which has an economic base ratio of 35% and an unemployment rate of 6% indicates that only **35% of the adult population is employed** while **6% of all people looking for work** cannot find a job. These ratios do not necessarily move in tandem. If the number of retirees increases, the unemployment rate can actually decrease while the economic base ratio will also decrease. A city could actually gain jobs and still show an increase in its unemployment ratio. It could also lose jobs and show a decrease in the unemployment ratio **if the number of people looking for work decreases**. Our economic base ratio ignores the anomalies of the unemployment ratio and purely looks at the number of jobs in a municipality compared to the number of people living in that municipality.

We compiled the economic base ratio for the top 100 American cities over 50 years. We also divided these cities into two categories: declining and vibrant. Cities that lost at least 20% of their population after 1960 were defined as declining cities. Vibrant cities either grew during this period or did not have an appreciable decline in population.

Finally, we looked at the average economic base of declining cities and vibrant cities during this period. Our findings are shown at the end of this chapter.

The difference in the economic base ratios between declining cities and vibrant cities was more than 10%. This finding is significant for several reasons. Remember, our economic base ratio is defined as the number of employed adults divided by the size of the adult population. In declining cities, the size of the adult population has decreased consistently for 50 years. If the number of jobs in declining cities remained constant or declined less than the adult population, our economic base ratio would actually increase.

In other words, our economic base ratio is an opposing indicator to changes in population. In vibrant cities, our economic base indicator would decrease as population increased unless the number of jobs increased at a greater rate than the population. The disparity in the economic base ratio indicators between declining and vibrant cities indicates that jobs are leaving at a faster rate than people in declining cities.

Finally, we reviewed the increase or decrease in the Economic Base Ratio for the top 100 U.S. Cities from 1970 to 2010. This increase or decrease illustrates if the job prospects for a resident in this city has improved or worsen during this time period. I'll define this ratio as the DEBR or the Delta in the Economic Base Ratio in this time. The DEBR is nearly triple in vibrant cities compared to declining cities. In other words, the job prospects for residents in vibrant cities have increased three times as much as declining cities.

Let's look at two cities in particular: Newark, New Jersey and Austin, Texas. Newark, a former industrial and

trading hub, is the largest city in New Jersey. The city originally gained prominence as a manufacturer of leather and
iron goods. In the 18th century, raw leather and iron ore were
transported from the interior of New Jersey by railroad or
the Morris Canal and processed into finished goods in the
many factories in Newark. Newark's strategic location near
the Atlantic Ocean made it a port city, and goods manufactured in Newark were transported throughout the United
States and Europe.

Between 1890 and 1930, the population of Newark
increased from 181,000 to 405,000 or an increase of more
than 200,000 in 40 years. Similar to many Northeastern and
Midwestern cities, the loss of manufacturing jobs in these cities led to the overall deterioration of the city and decrease in
population. Although Newark's decline began in the 1950's,
the stark turn Newark took was epitomized by the Newark
Race Riots of 1967. The causes of the riots were numerous. Some attribute them to the growing frustration of an
impoverished African-American community. Paradoxically,
the growth of the African-American community between the
1920's and 1960's occurred when Newark began losing, not
gaining, jobs. Today, Newark's population is at 273,000 or the
same number as in 1900.

Austin, unlike many other Texas cities, has growth that is
not attributed to oil or energy. Instead, Austin is one of the
high technology hubs of America. Austin, Texas' capital is

not a port city and did not have a substantial industrial base. In 1900, the population was an anemic 22,000 people. The placement of the University of Texas in Austin did provide for moderate growth, and the population increased to 150,000 by 1960.

Between 1960 and 2010, the population increased by more than 400%, from 150,000 to more than 700,000 people. Austin has been identified as one of the fastest growing cities in America. Many high tech companies such as Intel, Sun Microsystems, and Apple have major operations in the city. They were attracted to Austin by the multitudes of college graduated coming from the University of Texas. Whole Foods Supermarket, a leading provider of organic produce, is headquartered in Austin.

The recent histories of Austin, Texas and Newark, New Jersey are wildly divergent. While Austin has experienced explosive growth since the 1960's, Newark is still recovering from the race riots of 1967. Austin's population may approach 1,000,000 by 2020 while Newark's population has decreased substantially and is equal to its population in 1900.

The economic base ratios of Austin and Newark demonstrate the divergent paths of these two cities. Austin has an economic base ratio of 0.54. In other words, 54% of all adults are employed. In 1960, the ratio was only 0.37. The economic base ratio has increased by nearly 50% while the population has increased by 400% during this four decade period. Since our economic base ratio divides the number of employed adults by the number of adults in a municipality, the number of jobs in Austin must have increased even more than the increase in population to keep pace with the explosive increase in population. The number of employed adults increased from 70,000 to 350,000 between 1960 and 2010 or an increase of 500%.

The economic base ratio declined by 18% between 1960 and 2010 from a ratio of .40 to .33 in Newark. While 40% of all adults in Newark were working in 1960, only 33% of all adults were working by the year 2000. This decline occurred even though Newark lost nearly one-third of its population during this time. The weakening economic base ratio indicates that Newark's economic base must have declined even faster than its population. It did. The number of employed adults in Newark declined from 162,000 in 1960 to 90,000 in 2000, or nearly 50%.

*The bottom line is people follow jobs! This was the case in London in the 18th century and is the case now for American cities in the 21st century.*

Cities provide many recreational, social, and cultural diversions. Global cities such as Paris, Madrid, and Tokyo are known for their museums and nightlife. Millions come to New York for the Great White Way on Broadway.

Chicagoland is known for many things including Museum Mile and Lake Shore Drive. Although cities can be defined by its cultural institutions and tourist attractions, the basic purpose of all cities is to create greater economic opportunities for its residents. Cities grow and decline based on the economic opportunities it affords its residents. This is especially true today given the mobility of the population.

Declining cities are suffering because of the loss of jobs and consequential loss of population. Vibrant cities grow because they offer greater economic opportunities for their residents. Only rampant job creation can reverse the faith of declining cities. If job growth is not evident or obvious, declining cities must acknowledge that their population size is not an aberration but a direct consequence of the loss of jobs. Furthermore, the current population of a declining city is a factor of its jobs base and will not increase unless the economic base increases. Given the economic damage caused by the Great Recession, the current economic base and consequential population size of declining cities will not increase for the foreseeable future.

# E.

The following tables analyze the economic base ratio (EBR) for the top 100 U.S. Cities from 1970 to 2010. The information is separated by declining cities and vibrant cities.

The Economic Base Ratio is defined as follows

Economic Base Ratio (EBR) = Total Number of Employed Persons / Total Population Size

# Table I – Economic Base Ratio for Declining Cities

**Economic Base Ratio**

|  | 1970 EBR | 1980 EBR | 1990 EBR | 2000 EBR | 2010 EBR |
|---|---|---|---|---|---|
| **DECLINING CITIES** | | | | | |
| Detroit city, MI | 0.3668 | 0.3715 | 0.3282 | 0.3266 | 0.3485 |
| Chicago city, IL | 0.4232 | 0.4125 | 0.4114 | 0.4339 | 0.4214 |
| Philadelphia city, PA | 0.3953 | 0.3930 | 0.3710 | 0.4125 | 0.3856 |
| St. Louis city, MO | 0.3923 | 0.3728 | 0.3823 | 0.4073 | 0.4133 |
| Cleveland city, OH | 0.3862 | 0.3822 | 0.4566 | 0.3607 | 0.3774 |
| Baltimore city, MD | 0.3867 | 0.3908 | 0.3901 | 0.4282 | 0.3935 |
| Pittsburgh city, PA | 0.3673 | 0.3705 | 0.4026 | 0.4169 | 0.4329 |
| Buffalo city, NY | 0.3724 | 0.3717 | 0.3672 | 0.3997 | 0.3900 |
| Washington city, DC | 0.4542 | 0.4477 | 0.4712 | 0.5060 | 0.4626 |
| Cincinnati city, OH | 0.3774 | 0.3867 | 0.4137 | 0.4368 | 0.4546 |
| Milwaukee city, WI | 0.4082 | 0.4191 | 0.4488 | 0.4371 | 0.4294 |
| New Orleans city, LA | 0.3581 | 0.3527 | 0.3937 | 0.3777 | 0.3971 |
| Louisville city, KY | 0.3640 | 0.3913 | 0.4037 | 0.4298 | 0.4433 |
| Newark city, NJ | 0.4006 | 0.3588 | 0.3344 | 0.3840 | 0.3320 |
| Boston city, MA | 0.4186 | 0.4166 | 0.4570 | 0.5037 | 0.4855 |
| Minneapolis city, MN | 0.4399 | 0.4525 | 0.5144 | 0.5228 | 0.5435 |
| Rochester city, NY | 0.4076 | 0.4105 | 0.4180 | 0.4404 | 0.4184 |
| Birmingham city, AL | 0.3660 | 0.3817 | 0.4031 | 0.4148 | 0.4062 |
| Dayton city, OH | 0.3925 | 0.3988 | 0.3644 | 0.3908 | 0.4171 |
| Youngstown city, OH | 0.3527 | 0.3580 | 0.3401 | 0.3144 | 0.3494 |
| Gary city, IN | 0.3524 | 0.3572 | 0.3612 | 0.3403 | 0.3495 |
| Akron city, OH | 0.3787 | 0.3808 | 0.4011 | 0.4223 | 0.4576 |

| | | | | | |
|---|---|---|---|---|---|
| Flint city, MI | 0.3726 | 0.3618 | 0.3396 | 0.3342 | 0.3673 |
| Norfolk city, VA | 0.3242 | 0.3405 | 0.3852 | 0.4116 | 0.4223 |
| Atlanta city, GA | 0.4063 | 0.4222 | 0.4121 | 0.4454 | 0.4397 |
| Syracuse city, NY | 0.4072 | 0.4004 | 0.4144 | 0.4293 | 0.4125 |
| Hartford city, CT | 0.4527 | 0.4308 | 0.4173 | 0.4072 | 0.3489 |
| Jersey City, NJ | 0.3810 | 0.4040 | 0.3950 | 0.4579 | 0.4311 |
| Erie city, PA | 0.3511 | 0.3446 | 0.4109 | 0.4242 | 0.4314 |
| Albany city, NY | 0.4135 | 0.4257 | 0.4484 | 0.4943 | 0.4569 |
| Kansas City, MO | 0.4184 | 0.4223 | 0.4684 | 0.4874 | 0.4805 |
| Providence city, RI | 0.3872 | 0.4162 | 0.4197 | 0.4309 | 0.4010 |
| New Haven city, CT | 0.4144 | 0.4104 | 0.3991 | 0.4464 | 0.3994 |
| St. Paul city, MN | 0.4012 | 0.4189 | 0.4802 | 0.4904 | 0.4935 |
| South Bend city, IN | 0.3911 | 0.3969 | 0.4326 | 0.4507 | 0.4371 |
| Springfield city, MA | 0.3866 | 0.3947 | 0.4142 | 0.4162 | 0.3989 |
| Richmond city, VA | 0.4169 | 0.4184 | 0.4552 | 0.4743 | 0.4595 |
| Evansville city, IN | 0.3555 | 0.3957 | 0.4466 | 0.4635 | 0.4793 |
| Savannah city GA | 0.3503 | 0.3616 | 0.3919 | 0.4179 | 0.4173 |
| Bridgeport city, CT | 0.4042 | 0.4176 | 0.4191 | 0.4410 | 0.4080 |
| Worcester city, MA | 0.3902 | 0.4089 | 0.4389 | 0.4470 | 0.4491 |
| Des Moines city, IA | 0.4177 | 0.4331 | 0.4893 | 0.5174 | 0.5085 |
| Salt Lake City, UT | 0.3986 | 0.4109 | 0.4651 | 0.4743 | 0.5071 |
| Toledo city, OH | 0.3747 | 0.3943 | 0.3997 | 0.4248 | 0.4474 |
| Mobile city, AL | 0.3586 | 0.3447 | 0.4099 | 0.4194 | 0.4094 |

**AVERAGE EBR (1970 -2010)**          **42.48%**
**AVERAGE GROWTH in EBR (1970 - 2010)   3.51%**

# Table II – Total Change in Population in Declining Cities

## Total Change in Population
### 1970-2010

**DECLINING CITIES**

| | |
|---|---|
| Detroit city, MI | (718,874.00) |
| Chicago city, IL | (654,388.00) |
| Philadelphia city, PA | (484,962.00) |
| St. Louis city, MO | (401,837.00) |
| Cleveland city, OH | (397,647.00) |
| Baltimore city, MD | (287,870.00) |
| Pittsburgh city, PA | (269,769.00) |
| Buffalo city, NY | (240,111.00) |
| Washington city, DC | (191,897.00) |
| Cincinnati city, OH | (171,265.00) |
| Milwaukee city, WI | (144,350.00) |
| New Orleans city, LA | (142,851.00) |
| Louisville city, KY | (134,408.00) |
| Newark city, NJ | (131,674.00) |
| Boston city, MA | (108,056.00) |
| Minneapolis city, MN | (100,254.00) |
| Rochester city, NY | (98,838.00) |
| Birmingham city, AL | (98,067.00) |
| Dayton city, OH | (96,153.00) |
| Youngstown city, OH | (84,663.00) |
| Gary city, IN | (75,574.00) |
| Akron city, OH | (73,277.00) |
| Flint city, MI | (71,997.00) |
| Norfolk city, VA | (71,469.00) |
| Atlanta city, GA | (70,981.00) |

| | |
|---|---:|
| Syracuse city, NY | (68,732.00) |
| Hartford city, CT | (40,600.00) |
| Jersey City, NJ | (36,046.00) |
| Erie city, PA | (34,723.00) |
| Albany city, NY | (34,068.00) |
| Kansas City, MO | (33,994.00) |
| Providence city, RI | (33,880.00) |
| New Haven city, CT | (28,422.00) |
| St. Paul city, MN | (26,260.00) |
| South Bend city, IN | (24,656.00) |
| Springfield city, MA | (22,381.00) |
| Richmond city, VA | (22,168.00) |
| Evansville city, IN | (19,961.00) |
| Savannah city GA | (17,735.00) |
| Bridgeport city, CT | (17,219.00) |
| Worcester city, MA | (13,939.00) |
| Des Moines city, IA | (10,300.00) |
| Salt Lake City, UT | (7,711.00) |
| Toledo city, OH | (4,384.00) |
| Mobile city, AL | (3,864.00) |

# Table III – Economic Base Ratio in Vibrant Cities

## Economic Base Ratio

| | 1970 EBR | 1980 EBR | 1990 EBR | 2000 EBR | 2010 EBR |
|---|---|---|---|---|---|
| **VIBRANT CITIES** | | | | | |
| Yonkers city, NY | 0.4145 | 0.4348 | 0.4632 | 0.4758 | 0.4294 |
| Paterson city, NJ | 0.3949 | 0.3937 | 0.3824 | 0.4441 | 0.3522 |
| Seattle city, WA | 0.4157 | 0.4289 | 0.5104 | 0.5520 | 0.5718 |
| Spokane city, WA | 0.3559 | 0.3648 | 0.4165 | 0.4265 | 0.4568 |
| Grand Rapids city, MI | 0.3816 | 0.3862 | 0.4321 | 0.4545 | 0.4673 |
| Rockford city, IL | 0.4090 | 0.4151 | 0.4581 | 0.4678 | 0.4522 |
| Kansas City, KS | 0.3880 | 0.3993 | 0.4236 | 0.4316 | 0.4287 |
| Chattanooga city, TN | 0.3744 | 0.3908 | 0.4243 | 0.4455 | 0.4535 |
| Arlington CDP, VA | 0.4516 | 0.5088 | 0.5554 | 0.6354 | 0.6132 |
| Tampa city, FL | 0.3720 | 0.3827 | 0.4250 | 0.4699 | 0.4528 |
| Oakland city, CA | 0.3962 | 0.3913 | 0.4228 | 0.4388 | 0.4375 |
| Amarillo city, TX | 0.3866 | 0.4115 | 0.4826 | 0.4644 | 0.4672 |
| Shreveport city, LA | 0.3793 | 0.3741 | 0.4361 | 0.4003 | 0.4145 |
| San Francisco city, CA | 0.4563 | 0.4518 | 0.5088 | 0.5374 | 0.5510 |
| Jackson city, MS | 0.0881 | 0.3974 | 0.4508 | 0.4454 | 0.4217 |
| Fort Wayne city, IN | 0.3913 | 0.4151 | 0.4500 | 0.4923 | 0.4895 |
| Tacoma city WA | 0.3543 | 0.3508 | 0.3906 | 0.4296 | 0.4516 |
| Denver city, CO | 0.4024 | 0.4180 | 0.5022 | 0.5021 | 0.5129 |
| St. Petersburg city, FL | 0.3055 | 0.3211 | 0.3909 | 0.4609 | 0.4759 |
| Montgomery city, AL | 0.3645 | 0.3778 | 0.4129 | 0.4522 | 0.4364 |
| Miami city, FL | 0.4326 | 0.4466 | 0.4592 | 0.4226 | 0.3588 |

| | | | | | |
|---|---|---|---|---|---|
| Lubbock city, TX | 0.3794 | 0.3921 | 0.4835 | 0.4693 | 0.4764 |
| Baton Rouge city, LA | 0.3637 | 0.3738 | 0.4414 | 0.4362 | 0.4442 |
| Honolulu CDP, HI | 0.4003 | 0.4569 | 0.5072 | 0.5357 | 0.4659 |
| Madison city, W | 0.4205 | 0.4414 | 0.5347 | 0.5665 | 0.5859 |
| Omaha city, NE | 0.4015 | 0.4079 | 0.4642 | 0.5017 | 0.5114 |
| Wichita city, KS | 0.3889 | 0.4014 | 0.5025 | 0.4952 | 0.4836 |
| Lincoln city, NE | 0.4243 | 0.4565 | 0.5317 | 0.5538 | 0.5606 |
| Greensboro city, NC | 0.4244 | 0.4349 | 0.4865 | 0.5449 | 0.5119 |
| Corpus Christi city, TX | 0.3343 | 0.3582 | 0.4423 | 0.4293 | 0.4307 |
| Long Beach city, CA | 0.3928 | 0.4050 | 0.4572 | 0.4705 | 0.4109 |
| Tulsa city, OK | 0.3973 | 0.4092 | 0.5011 | 0.4890 | 0.4861 |
| Memphis city, TN | 0.3753 | 0.3840 | 0.4172 | 0.4388 | 0.4313 |
| Portland city, OR | 0.4030 | 0.4089 | 1.1897 | 0.5007 | 0.5219 |
| Fort Worth city, TX | 0.3917 | 0.4121 | 0.4703 | 0.4658 | 0.4503 |
| Oklahoma City, OK | 0.4028 | 0.4177 | 0.4626 | 0.4756 | 0.4684 |
| Sacramento city, CA | 0.4183 | 0.3734 | 0.4122 | 0.4390 | 0.4177 |
| New York city, NY | 0.4257 | 0.4049 | 0.4130 | 0.4453 | 0.4094 |
| Columbus city, OH | 0.3863 | 0.4066 | 0.4639 | 0.5143 | 0.5273 |
| Albuquerque city, NM | 0.3600 | 0.3706 | 0.4599 | 0.4911 | 0.4858 |
| Tucson city, AZ | 0.3393 | 0.3503 | 0.4353 | 0.4492 | 0.4480 |
| El Paso city, TX | 0.3103 | 0.3199 | 0.3716 | 0.3862 | 0.3713 |
| Fresno city, CA | 0.3656 | 0.3560 | 0.4297 | 0.3946 | 0.3738 |
| Indianapolis city, IN | 0.4071 | 0.4040 | 0.4624 | 0.5038 | 0.5020 |
| Charlotte city, NC | 0.4178 | 0.4395 | 0.5128 | 0.5480 | 0.5283 |
| Nashville city, TN | 0.3930 | 0.4100 | 0.4721 | 0.5194 | 0.5122 |
| Austin city, TX | 0.3771 | 0.4110 | 0.5085 | 0.5285 | 0.5484 |
| Dallas city, TX | 0.4232 | 0.4437 | 0.5148 | 0.5083 | 0.4621 |
| Jacksonville city, FL | 0.3949 | 0.3816 | 0.4251 | 0.4824 | 0.4763 |

| | | | | | |
|---|---|---|---|---|---|
| San Antonio city, TX | 0.3224 | 0.3449 | 0.3980 | 0.4235 | 0.4321 |
| San Diego city, CA | 0.3541 | 0.3620 | 0.4301 | 0.4939 | 0.4696 |
| San Jose city, CA | 0.3655 | 0.3643 | 0.4907 | 0.5221 | 0.4883 |
| Phoenix city, AZ | 0.3644 | 0.3972 | 0.4662 | 0.4901 | 0.4629 |
| Houston city, TX | 0.3879 | 0.4187 | 0.5188 | 0.4839 | 0.4404 |
| Los Angeles city, CA | 0.4098 | 0.4107 | 0.4705 | 0.4797 | 0.4148 |

**AVERAGE EBR (1970 -2010)          47.03%**
**AVERAGE GROWTH in EBR (1970 - 2010)   8.86%**

# Table IV – Change in Population in Vibrant Cities (1970-2010)

| | Total Change in Population 1970-2010 |
|---|---|
| **VIBRANT CITIES** | |
| Yonkers city, NY | 5,452.00 |
| Paterson city, NJ | 5,559.00 |
| Seattle city, WA | 6,287.00 |
| Spokane city, WA | 14,021.00 |
| Grand Rapids city, MI | 20,487.00 |
| Rockford city, IL | 23,409.00 |
| Kansas City, KS | 24,965.00 |
| Chattanooga city, TN | 25,545.00 |
| Arlington CDP, VA | 26,052.00 |
| Tampa city, FL | 28,477.00 |
| Oakland city, CA | 31,936.00 |
| Amarillo city, TX | 35,658.00 |
| Shreveport city, LA | 35,773.00 |
| San Francisco city, CA | 36,417.00 |
| Jackson city, MS | 39,834.00 |
| Fort Wayne city, IN | 43,951.00 |
| Tacoma city WA | 45,577.00 |
| Denver city, CO | 60,749.00 |
| St. Petersburg city, FL | 66,934.00 |
| Montgomery city, AL | 67,175.00 |
| Miami city, FL | 70,782.00 |
| Lubbock city, TX | 70,873.00 |
| Baton Rouge city, LA | 75,399.00 |
| Honolulu CDP, HI | 77,463.00 |

| | |
|---|---:|
| Madison city, W | 81,348.00 |
| Omaha city, NE | 88,409.00 |
| Wichita city, KS | 89,586.00 |
| Lincoln city, NE | 97,060.00 |
| Greensboro city, NC | 104,317.00 |
| Corpus Christi city, TX | 109,764.00 |
| Long Beach city, CA | 117,354.00 |
| Tulsa city, OK | 131,364.00 |
| Memphis city, TN | 152,576.00 |
| Portland city, OR | 156,445.00 |
| Fort Worth city, TX | 178,426.00 |
| Oklahoma City, OK | 181,879.00 |
| Sacramento city, CA | 215,351.00 |
| New York city, NY | 226,294.00 |
| Columbus city, OH | 240,154.00 |
| Albuquerque city, NM | 247,418.00 |
| Tucson city, AZ | 273,807.00 |
| El Paso city, TX | 286,975.00 |
| Fresno city, CA | 293,723.00 |
| Indianapolis city, IN | 305,612.00 |
| Charlotte city, NC | 339,264.00 |
| Nashville city, TN | 374,650.00 |
| Austin city, TX | 470,017.00 |
| Dallas city, TX | 508,896.00 |
| Jacksonville city, FL | 534,587.00 |
| San Antonio city, TX | 556,928.00 |
| San Diego city, CA | 650,176.00 |
| San Jose city, CA | 690,747.00 |
| Phoenix city, AZ | 881,875.00 |
| Houston city, TX | 1,015,412.00 |
| Los Angeles city, CA | 1,215,805.00 |

# CHAPTER III

# THE TICKING TIME BOMB – MUNICIPAL PENSIONS?

Coming to terms with and paying promised retiree benefits remains one of the biggest areas of financial weakness among American cities. While pension promises demand billions from city budgets, it remains a topic that is poorly understood by the general public. Outside of a handful of politicians, the most informed and passionate partisans on the subject tend to be pension members fighting to keep existing benefits or fiscal conservatives concerned with the current level of retirement promises for municipal workers. This discussion between fiscal conservatives and pension recipients is made even more complicated by the demographic changes overtaking America with the advent and aging of the baby boomer generation. Due to the increasing number of pension recipients and the longer life expectations of recipients, municipalities and states will have an increasingly difficult time honoring existing commitments to pension recipients and balancing their budgets.

## A.

In 2014, the nation watched with baited breath as Detroit dropped to its financial knees. Perhaps no group was quite as nervous as the 20,000 municipal retirees depending on city pension payments for their ongoing livelihood. Detroit's infamy for unplanned shrinkage and budgetary mismanagement was just setting in. And a pending court decision on pension cuts as part of Chapter 9 bankruptcy proceedings could forever change the lives of these 20,000 and future pensioners. The proposed cuts included unprecedented decreases to cash payouts, slashed health care benefits and even a debt that hit retirees by surprise.

The plight of struggling and frustrated public pensioners was all over the news by late 2015. It turned out that even Michigan's constitutional protection for public pensions was no match for the desperate times. Former city workers like Belinda Myers- Florence and Cecily McClellan thought their decades of public employment were safely behind them and that nothing could disrupt the benefits they earned over time. The court's Chapter 9 ruling allowed Detroit to cut payments to all city pensioners outside of police and firemen by a rate of 4.5 percent. In a city where the average pension is $19,000 per year, that is a decrease of around $855 from annual incomes below the poverty level for family of three.

The drop in payment could be one less month's rent or ten fewer trips to the grocery store.

The cut in straight pension payments was just one of four retiree-related items approved in the bankruptcy package. Pensioners including police and firefighters also lost much of their promised health benefits and the 2.25 percent annual cost of living adjustment (COLA). In a final painful blow, the court decided that about 11,000 retirees would have to return interest overpayments they collected in a municipal savings fund over the duration of their employment. For some like Elaine Williams, that debt totals $10,000, which she must repay via deductions from her monthly pension checks for the next 17 years. David Espie, a former Department of Public Works employee, told the Detroit Metro Times that he would be repaying the city $75,000 and that he felt "betrayed."

Ms. McClellan worked with Detroit's health department for 18 years and after the court ruling, the cost to fund her own health care jumped to around $500 monthly.

In an interview she said, "…this will be devastating. Many people who thought they had a decent nest egg are going to find themselves living in poverty." Myers- Florence told the Detroit Metro Times, "When I take the time to talk to people and tell them what's really happening, they say they had no idea."

The loss of promised health care benefits was easily the biggest blow to retirees. In an interview with the Detroit Journalism Cooperative, pensioner William Davis said, "After 36 years I thought my wife and myself would receive health care the rest of our life, and it's gone now. Public employees historically work for less hourly pay because they have a promise for better benefits and better promise of better pension in retirement and now, like I say I was 10 years into retirement and all of the sudden the bankruptcy occurred, and we mainly we lost the healthcare benefit. The whole thing was just wrong and as far as we're concerned it was illegal."

## B.

A brief look at the arc of pension development provides some insight into how this progressive endeavor could evolve into a ticking time bomb. According to the Employee Benefits Research Institute, the root of public employee retirement systems can be traced back to 1857. That year, the first government employees in America to be covered by a state or local retirement system were the New York City police. Throughout the late 1800s, businesses and governments developed an interest in extending economic benefits to employees beyond their active working years. While public school teachers and health and safety professionals were the focus of the earliest retirement systems, the first half of the 20th century ushered in the establishment of retirement plans for a range of professions at both state and local levels.

In the 1930s, the federal government made its first mark on developing pension plan systems around the country. The Social Security Act of 1935 was the first national level retirement policy and yet it excluded public employees at the local level. This omission came in large part because of Congress's struggle with the constitutional question of taxing states and cities. Plus, trends of the previous 70 years led to the coverage of large numbers of public employees in state and local programs. By the 1950s, however, governments without retirement plans could opt into federal coverage with the

Social Security Administration. After some back and forth, Congress made Social Security coverage mandatory for state and local public employees not already protected by a local retirement plan. Today, new government employees may opt out of Social Security payments and benefits if they enroll in a public retirement plans operating outside of the Social Security system.

State and local retirement systems experienced decades of expansion and subsequent consolidation since the 1960s. Pension membership levels and plan quantities rose rapidly throughout the '60s and '70s. Public employment at all levels ticked upward in response to increased need for government services. And greater numbers of people were drawn to public employment by generous pay and the promise of union protection. However, the growth in public pension membership has slowed markedly since the 1980s. During the 70s and 80s, an effort to consolidate public plans meant that smaller municipal plans were usurped into larger, often state level plans. The goal was to create efficiencies through economies of scale. The result was a reduced total number of pension systems.

The Congressional Budget Office reports that there are now 2,550 state and local government retirement systems. State-administered pensions cover roughly 90 percent of public plan members. Many city government employees, particularly public school teachers, are covered by state-level plans. City plans typically take responsibility for covering police and firefighters, as well as general municipal employees. Social Security supplements the coverage of about 70 percent of public employees at the state and local levels.

Understanding city pension funding challenges involves a look at the composition of retirement plan assets and liabilities. Retirement plans are forward funded. That is, money goes into the system in advance to cover benefits earned by workers over the course of their employment. This system of funding can require complicated calculations of future costs and requires the aid of financial actuaries to determine inputs and fund values. However, forward funding is in theory the way for workers to save now for retirement and avoid burdening future generations. In conjunction with taxpayer-funded government contributions, each cohort covers the cost of its own future retirement. This should guarantee that funds are available as pensions come up for payment.

The inputs and outputs of pension systems can be understood in rather simple terms. Inputs into the system are comprised of contributions from employers and workers, combined with returns on market investments. For municipal workers, the employers are either city or state government. The simple equation for municipal pension plan funding is as follows:

C + I − B + E (C)ontributions + (I)nvestment returns = (B)enefits earned + administrative (E)xpenses

The left side of this equation covers inputs or assets belonging to the pension plans, while the right side includes retirement system costs or liabilities. "C" represents contributions from government and workers, "I" represents income from invested funds, "B" represents benefits earned and outgoing and "E" represents a fund's administrative expenses.

Ideally, a system is fully funded and thus both sides of the equation are balanced. This means that assets should be equal to or greater than the value of pension obligations in order for the system to work. However, in the event that either pension funding drops or the payouts increase, unfunded liabilities and underfunding of the entire system can become a problem. Unfunded liability arises when contributions and investment income fail to cover all administrative costs and retiree benefits payments. This can happen for a number of reasons:

- Delaying contributions due to funding limitations
- Increased benefits due to more pensioners or pensioners living longer than expected lives
- Stock market/investment performance

A pension plan's funding level can only improve when the value of assets grows faster than its liabilities. Cities often make the uncomfortable choice to delay full contributions in favor of public spending with more urgent timing such as infrastructure improvements or hiring more workers. Repeatedly making this choice leaves a lasting impression on the health of pension funds. Imbalance might also occur if additional benefits are offered without the requisite employee contribution to pay for the increased costs. A disruption or drop in the stock market can wreak havoc on expected returns and thus necessitate higher contributions from both cities and plan members.

How do cities know the level of contributions needed to keep a pension system healthy and functioning? The first step is to calculate a plan's value. The market value of a plan is the sale value of all investment assets (stocks, bonds, mutual fund, etc.) as of a particular date. Contribution levels are then determined by subtracting the total plan cost from the pension's investment assets. Expected city contributions are equal to the pension plan cost minus investment assets and expected individual member and state contributions. Going back to the basic funding equation, the city, plan member and state contributions plus investment assets should equal the total plan cost in order for a system to be considered fully funded. However, even a system that is funded at 100% should be receiving contributions toward both the normal cost and accrued liabilities annually. These costs continue to build each year and a fiscally healthy plan requires that municipalities maintain contributions to cover both the normal costs and any possible gap developing between the plan value and its liabilities.

Here is a sample analysis of municipal pension contribution requirements from the Florida Public Pension Trustees Association:

Figure 1.    (Source: Florida Public Pension Trustees Association)

## C.

**A** composite of pension funding around the country shows that undisciplined city contributions are indeed widespread. Cities everywhere are trying to avoid the long-term fiscal consequences of off-kilter retirement systems. The Pew Charitable Trusts studied local pension health among 61 of America's cities, using a sample group including the most populous city in each state plus any others with upwards of half a million people. The study results shined a bright light on a national embarrassment. The analysis showed a combined funding gap of approximately $218 billion between benefits promised to municipal retirees and the actual funds cities had laid-away to meet those obligations. By 2009, roughly $100 billion of pension obligations were unfunded at the city level, with another $118 billion of promised but unfunded health and life insurance, and other benefits. These long-term promises are standard for current and future public sector retirees but not many cities are saving appropriately to fund the long-term costs. Unfunded retiree health care obligations dwarf even that of pension commitments. Cities in the Pew study only managed to have 6 percent of municipal non-pension benefit obligations on reserve.

Most public employees, including the people who provide the most essential health, safety and education functions, trust that they can safely rely on their pensions and other promised benefits when their time as public servants comes to an end. For many, pensions are the only safety net that will apply upon retirement because they opted out of Social Security. Members make their contractual contributions to the pension system over the lifetime of their career and expect that cities are doing the same. However, if the cost of maintaining a pension fund increases, this requires some balancing to raise the inputs in the funding equation [Remember C + I = B + E (C)ontributions + (I)nvestment returns = (B)enefits earned + administrative (E)xpenses ]. Cities could prioritize pension obligations over other municipal needs, such as infrastructure or education spending. This is highly unpopular and politically unwise. Alternately, new or higher taxes could be levied to generate the necessary financing. Either way, this puts the soundness of the public retirement system in competition with the rest of the city's needs if benefit levels and employee contributions remain unchanged.

The funding of public retirement systems is a significant budgetary burden that cities bear. On average, the cities in Pew's study were spending approximately 9 percent of tax income on retirement plan contributions alone. This rate is expected to stretch upward as the median U.S. age increases and more baby boomers are hitting retirement. And while the financial stress is a municipal problem, the implications are unbounded in terms of levels of government. Perhaps Detroit is the most obvious example of city crisis that required state intervention to avoid an implosion of its public pension plan and promised benefits. Select cities are legally obligated to fund their pension obligations at 100 percent. This mandate can come from the state legislatures or a municipal body. However, many cities are unencumbered by such directives. As a result, these same cities can and do find other budget allocations and this pushes the necessary future pension contributions even higher.

Of the 61 cities analyzed by Pew, four stood out as having the worst pension plan funding positions at 50 percent or less. Charleston, WV came in at rock bottom with merely 24 percent of its municipal pension obligations funded. This was followed by Providence, RI and Omaha, NE at 42 percent and 43 percent funding respectively. Portland, OR was measured as having funded only half of its liabilities. And while each of these cities has enacted measures to address their sizable gaps, closing these gaps is a formidable challenge.

America's largest cities make up the lion's share of local public pension debt. Pew's study reported over 70 percent of unfunded municipal pension liabilities belonging to New York City, Los Angeles, Houston, Chicago and Philadelphia. The funding levels in these five cities ranged from 89 percent in the case of Los Angeles to only 52 percent in Chicago.

The level of fiscal discipline across cities is as diverse as the cities themselves. Some cities are well prepared to meet their pension promises, while others are in rather dangerous territory. The city of Milwaukee is setting the standard for successful pension funding. By the end of 2009, Milwaukee could effectively fund 113 percent of its retirement obligations through accumulated funds. A handful of cities find themselves in a situation where less than half of their retiree obligations are funded. Pew found Charleston, West Virginia in the direst position with the means to fund only 24 percent of its liabilities.

A separate in-depth study by Joshua D. Rauh illustrates how the gap in municipal pension funding continued to widen despite the stock market rebound in the last 6 years. From 2009 to 2013, the S&P 500 increased in value by more than 75% and the Dow Jones Industrial Most pension funds experienced annual rates of return on their investments in excess of 7.5%-8%. During this same period, however, New York, Chicago and Philadelphia actually experienced an increase in their unfunded pension obligations. Cities including Atlanta and Baltimore saw a slight decrease in unfunded retirement liabilities but the gap does not appear to be closing for the majority of municipalities. This is counterintuitive as investment returns go up and thus assets are increasing. But despite robust market returns, benefits payments continue to eclipse city government contributions to the pension system.

Benefits payments have increased roughly 22% from 2009 to 2013 while contributions to pension systems have

gone up by about 33%. Even with both municipal governments and employees putting more into the system, the
benefit payout increases continue to outstrip gains in contributions. And even as contributions have risen, the percent
of actuarially required contributions (ARC) paid into municipal systems averaged only 78% from 2008 to 2012. In other
words, even strong returns on investment assets are not sufficient to close this gap.

The proportion of city revenues going toward pension contributions varies widely. According to Kiewiet &
McCubbins, average government funding of state and local
retirement plans around the U.S. sits at approximately 5.7%
of revenues. Rauh's study showed that on the higher end of
the spectrum Philadelphia pension contributions equal nearly
20% of city revenues. New York's contributions total over
15% of revenue, and contributions in the cities of Baltimore
and Chicago lie between 12% and 10%. While the ratio of
benefit payouts ranges from 16% to 9% in these cities, the
revenue needed in the event of asset failure is eye-opening. In
the case of Chicago, nearly 50% of the city's revenue would
be necessary to cover the pension obligation shortfall should
funds run dry. In other words, 50 cents of every dollar raised
from taxes is needed in Chicago to fund unfunded pension
liabilities.

Total unfunded pension liabilities from 2009 to 2013
increased steadily while lower interest rates have driven the

cost of maintaining retirement packages upward. As of 2013, New York City, Baltimore and Philadelphia held unfunded pension obligations amounting to between four and six times their tax revenue base. Meanwhile, Chicago faces a situation where pension liabilities amounted to more than ten times the existing tax revenue base. The average 2013 unfunded pension obligations calculated on a per-household basis reached $66,900 in Chicago, $55,600 in New York and approximately $20,000 in both Philadelphia and Baltimore.

## D.

**A** basic Internet search combining the words "Illinois" and "pensions" generates hundreds of headlines warning of fiscal calamity. Chicago serves as a stark example of how municipal pension management can escape the control of local government. Successive mayors have faced the excruciating choice between public school closures and shorting city pension contributions. Even when pension payments win out, the city fails to meet the required contribution levels. Unfortunately, Chicago's neglect of its retirement obligations is not unique in Illinois. Excluding Chicago, there are approximately 650 municipal pension funds in the state, most of which are woefully short on plan assets. This means that payments to current retirees and promises to future retirees are at risk of being cut for lack of money, even as governments sacrifice more to pump additional resources into pension funds.

The public pension systems in Springfield have been identified as being in a state of "critical risk" by the Illinois Policy Institute and are representative of a bigger problem that plagues so many Illinois cities. Springfield has four main pension plans under its purview: the Illinois Municipal Retirement Fund - Regular (IMRF) and Sheriff's Law Enforcement Personnel (SLEP), the Police Pension Fund and the Springfield Firefighters' Pension Fund. Fortunately for Springfield, the

Teachers' Retirement System of the State of Illinois (TRS) covers the responsibility of public school employee pensions. Unfortunately for those teachers, TRS is only 42 percent funded and $70 billion of its $75 billion accrued liability is owed to members who are already in retirement. But let us get back to the situation in Springfield.

All Springfield municipal pensions are structured such that the city contributes the lion's share of funds. In each case employees contribute at a fixed rate predetermined by state statute and the city contributes a rate determined annually by fund auditors. Active employees, excluding police and firemen are required to contribute 4.5 percent of their salaries and the city of Springfield contributed 16 percent of payroll value in 2014. Members of the Springfield police must contribute 9.91 percent of their salary to the pension fund, while firefighters must contribute 9.455 percent of base earnings to their pension. Police and firefighter plans require that Springfield "contribute the remaining amounts necessary to finance the Plan" as determined by a qualified auditor. In 2014, Springfield's share of police and firefighter pension payments were 52.67 percent and 65 percent of payroll respectively, compared to 16 percent of IMRF payroll. This means that contributions by police and firefighters are fixed to their salaries, while the city contributions are at the mercy of all other costs that inform the calculation of plan expenses. This helps explain why municipal responsibilities have increased so aggressively in comparison to employee inputs. Springfield budget records reveal that in 2014, the city's annual contribution to public retirement plans totaled more than $29.5 million. This amount was nearly triple the contribution size in the year 2000.

All Springfield municipal pension funds are defined benefit plans that may be promising unrealistic packages for the future. Police who reach the age of 50 with at least 20 years of service behind them are guaranteed half of their last annual salary upon retirement. For each year of employment beyond 20, the salary amount increases by another 2.5 percent annually for up to 10 years (or 30 years in total). Firefighters with the same service levels are promised no less than 50 percent and no more than 75 percent of their final annual salary in retirement. Beyond this, Springfield has promised to budget for and fund anticipated salary increases of 5 percent annually, 4 percent inflation and a 3 percent cost of living adjustments (COLA). All of these obligations culminate in a bill that the city of Springfield cannot pay in full over the long term.

Springfield has failed to keep pace with rising costs. This is evident when looking at current pension funding ratios. By the close of fiscal year 2014, the municipal firefighter retirement plan was funded at only 47 percent with an unfunded liability of $124 million. The police pension plan was funded at 54 percent of the amount required to meet promised obligations, creating a gap of $104.4 million. The city's IMRF has $94 million of unfunded liabilities and a slightly higher funding rate of 64 percent. On top of these unfunded obligations, Springfield has a $376 million debt behemoth looming with less than 25 percent of funding on reserve: the municipal retiree health plan.

The urgency of these liabilities is heightened by the composition of pension plan membership. The Police Pension Fund has 246 active employee members and 225 retirees currently receiving benefits. The Springfield firefighters pension covers 217 active workers and 241 pensioners. As a whole, city pensions now have more retirees receiving benefits payments than active members with 463 active and 466 retired. Springfield expects another 25 percent of the fire department to retire by the 2019. The growing costs from automatic increases in benefits are borne by a smaller group of workers, which passes additional responsibility onto the general public. As people live longer, this pattern of more retirees than active workers will continue in Springfield and throughout American cities. Budget constraints deter cities like Springfield from hiring to replace lost or retiring workers, further straining pension plan financing.

In an effort to deliver on promised benefits, Springfield has levied and allocated ever-larger amounts to fund the pension system. Nearly 25 percent of the city's entire budget went toward pension costs in 2012. Property taxes are the primary revenue source for city pension payments and Illinois already has some of the highest property taxes in the nation.

Despite annual increases in municipal property tax income, Springfield is not able to generate enough to cover its total pension obligations. Contributions to the city pension plans equal more than 136 percent of property tax revenue. This not only precludes other uses for property tax income, it necessitates the taking from other public services and needs.

*Consolidation of assistance*

Public safety and infrastructure present urgent public needs and Springfield must choose between these areas of public interest and the pension bill. 2014 crime data for the city of Springfield shows the city as above the national and regional average in terms of crimes per 100,000 residents. Where the US average for violent crime was 203 per 100,000, Springfield had a rate of 567 per 100,000. Property crimes in the same year averaged 232 per 100,000 people nationally whereas Springfield had 381 per 100,000 people. This is happening against a backdrop of a shrinking police force. Springfield had 1.98 full-time police officers per 1,000 residents in 2014 versus an Illinois average of 3.28 officers per 1,000 residents. In 2010, Springfield was named one of America's most dangerous cities by the Wall Street Journal. Still, the police and fire pensions alone consumed 88 percent of the city's tax levy in 2014, leaving little revenue for anything else. Growing public safety allocations will require alternate funding.

In 2013, the director of Illinois Public Works addressed the aldermen of Springfield. He told them in no uncertain terms that the city's critical infrastructure was crumbling and that necessary improvements to streets, sidewalks and storm water management systems would take approximately $86.6 million from 2014 to 2017. He followed this with a recommendation that Springfield commit an additional $22.5 million annually going forward to keep the infrastructure in acceptable condition. Meanwhile, the total municipal public works expenditure in 2014-15 was only $33 million, more than $8 million less than the previous fiscal year. Springfield infrastructure continues to wait for the requisite servicing while pension debt that is being serviced at sky-high rates continues to gobble up more resources.

E.

**P**ension obligations are a problem for cities large and small. Requisite annual contributions on the part of city governments can easily fall behind. Meanwhile, stewards of city budgets face little real pressure to keep funding levels up to par. Over time, the inability to fully fund pensions will leave cities with no choice but to reduce the long-term benefits promised to employees. Money needed to make sensible pension contributions already usurps resources that could be used for essential services such as public health, safety and infrastructure. This trend will only increase in severity if difficult changes are not made.

The problem has ballooned in magnitude even as the stock market and overall economy creep toward recovery following the Great Recession. Many analysts agree that residents of every city need to demand transparency and more detailed information around pension obligations if there is any hope of solving the funding problem. However, almost no powerful incentives exist to drive politicians to prioritize long-view funding policies. On the contrary, city executives are more often rewarded for shortsighted budget choices that push growing pension obligations further into the future.

Current political and economic powers reward the choice to underfund municipal pension systems. The problem is rooted in years of failure to properly contribute to pension funds. During the tech boom of the 90s, cities throughout California were cavalier in the increasing of pension benefits without tying such increases to greater government or employee contributions. Political budget allocations are the primary culprit for ongoing funding failures. Pension contributions must compete with all other municipal needs and urgent voter items typically win the prize. In the case of Springfield, high-level pension expenditures are still not enough to close the gap. However, most cities are not allocating similar levels of public funding to pension system payments. Spending on pensions is in essence invisible to the public unless they scour municipal balance sheets and hence becomes a low-reward action, albeit prudent and necessary. Additionally, those affected by the public pension system are generally not pushing for higher government contributions because such allocations compete with funding for salaries and other current benefits such as health care. Even actual plan investments are at the mercy of municipal level politics. This can lead to poor portfolio choices and investment decisions based on biases or favoritism.

Pressure from possible credit rating downgrades and even legal action are often not enough to induce proper contribution action. Credit markets typically only help create pressure for better funding when a pension plan reaches a crisis low. In most jurisdictions pension participants cannot legally claim harm unless or until a fund actually runs out of money. The failure to fund a system cannot be tested until benefits come due that a city cannot pay. Laws vary widely from state to state and city to city in terms of what benefits are protected and at what time. This creates a disincentive on the part of leaders who are uncertain of how their attempts at addressing pension problems will be viewed by the legal system. Even when state constitutions mandate annual pension funding levels, cities can and do ignore these legal parameters and there are no consequences for the subsequent misallocation of budgets.

As discussed in previous chapters, three of the most critical underpinnings of crumbling municipal finance include collapsing industries and lost jobs, aging populations and outward migration leading to shrinking cities. These factors culminate in a grim and untenable financial situation for affected cities. We see these trends in play at varying degrees in all shrinking cities. Ballooning pension obligations, sizable portions of which are unfunded, strain these cities even further.

Cities such as Detroit and Baltimore have experienced a reduction in their tax base as the proportion of low-wage workers creeps up and a hollowed-out city further complicates the task of funding essential services plus future pension benefits.

More cities are grappling with the struggle between essential services for residents and benefits, namely health care obligations. Too often, governments are electing to divert funding from basic community needs, rather than take on more debt or increase taxes to cover benefit obligations.

Of course, the number of retirees collecting pension payments does not decrease in proportion with the shrinkage that may be taking place in a city. If retirees relocate they still receive benefits from the city in which they worked. This pulls money out of the community in terms of allocation as well as consumer spending and tax receipts. Shrinking cities with aging populations have the compound problem of a smaller tax base plus the demand for more services necessitated by the elderly.

American demographic trends are a critical part of the pension-funding story. The baby boomer generation is creating a retiree cohort of a size never before seen by this country. This shift is setting the stage for an even bigger problem as the retiree-to-worker ratio grows. Nationally, the number of pensioners is approximately 50% of the current number of active public workers. The 2014 Annual Survey of Public Pensions reveals a total state and local pension membership of 19.6 million, of which 9.5 million currently receive benefits payments. The bounty of boomers in the form of better health and longevity than previous generations has cities paying out benefits for years, sometimes decades beyond projection.

No simple fix exists for the pension crisis. And any possible fix will trigger a host of political, financial and/or social costs. The good news is that economists and policy experts offer options that could reverse the funding gap trend and ultimately eliminate it. Where there is political will, there is a way - or a combination of ways. Proposed approaches include changing benefit structures, amending benefit parameters and adjusting member contributions.

### Change the Structure

Structural changes are recommended as the only long-term solutions to the funding gap but they are sure to incite staunch opposition and require political gymnastics.

Structural changes include moving public employees to alternative plans such as individual 401K retirement plans, pooled defined-contribution plans and deferred-annuity plans. Any one of these structural changes would effectively end the accumulation of new unfunded pension obligations. Deferred-annuity plans are arguably the strongest of the options because the responsibility for maintaining the pension plan is transferred to an insurer, leaving cities virtually free of the financial burden. Securing public employee support for changes that trigger more fees and in some cases reduced benefits is predictably challenging. The topic of changing pension structures is often a political third rail. Thus, while it gives cities the best chance of changing financial fortunes, rare is the politician with the stomach to propose such a strategy.

## Amend Benefit Parameters

Altering the parameters of pension plans creates relief of a different sort. These could include increasing the retirement age and reducing employee benefits. Pushing the retirement age up clearly helps cities by reducing the number of years that pensioners receive their payouts. Decreasing cost of living adjustments (COLAs) is another option, which reduces the payout increases after employees enter retirement. This option essentially provides instant reductions in overall city liability. However, this is unpopular because it leaves pensioners vulnerable to inflation. One criticism is that the current calculation for pension-related COLAs is not in fact tied to actual inflation rates, thus creating a situation where COLAs increase at a higher rate. One recommendation is to tether all COLAs to the actual rate of inflation going forward. In the view of city pension holders, however, pulling back on COLAs runs counter to the spirit of honoring earned benefits and is tantamount to a broken promise to retirees.

## Active Members Pay More

Requiring larger contributions from current employees or those yet to retire is yet another potential remedy for cities. This type of change disproportionately affects younger employees, making it an easier political battle to win. No city currently has a deferred-benefits plan with contribution levels that are sufficient to both cover the cost of new pension obligations and pay down its existing promises.

Release the Burden

Buyouts and Chapter 9 bankruptcy are other possible mechanisms to handle pension gaps that cities have little hope of closing. Lump sum buyouts may be more attractive to some workers who can then find other financial vehicles for their earned benefits. Filing for Chapter 9 bankruptcy would present an opportunity for hard restructuring of pension packages. Ultimately, it is informed citizens who will change the conversation by engaging politicians and holding officials accountable for city pension obligations.

CHAPTER IV

# THE BENEFITS OF PLANNED SHRINKAGE

## A.

**S**alah James is a mother of two young children in Detroit. Raymond and Saida James are five and nine, respectively. Originally from Uganda, she fervently believes in the American Dream and works hard to ensure that her children receive a good education in the Detroit Public School System. Her family emigrated from Uganda to Detroit to seek a better life and escape the poverty and tyranny of Uganda in the 1990's. She completed high school in Detroit and, in her early twenties, married a former Marine.

She does not allow her children to watch television during the week and she ensures that their homework is completed every night. As an African immigrant, she is able to tap into the African community in Detroit for support and guidance. Like most immigrants, she relies on her extended family to assist with childcare and financial support.

This is helpful because Detroit is not an easy place to raise children. James' husband recently passed at age 45 due to complications from drug and alcohol dependency. She works sporadically as a nurse's aide. With a stated unemployment rate of 27%, she is lucky to have a job. However, she is determined to create a better life for her children.

Unfortunately, Detroit does not or cannot take James' children's education as seriously as she does. In math tests developed by the U.S. Department of Education and the National Center for Educational Statistics, Detroit's fourth and eighth graders posted the lowest math scores in the nation. Secretary of Education, Arne Duncan, has dubbed the Detroit Public School System as "national disgrace." These tests scores represent a culmination of several years of turbulent times for the Detroit Public School System.

Former Governor Jennifer Granholm of Michigan appointed Robert Bobb as the special administrator of the Detroit Public School System (DPS) in 2008 after the state was forced to assume control of the school system. He closed more than 80 schools and laid off 1,000 employees in an attempt to correct previous mismanagement. The more egregious forms of corruption included payroll checks to ghost employees. DPS continues to flirt with a bankruptcy filing and the teachers recently staged a "sick-in". The teachers union coordinated many teachers taking sick days at the same time to protest DPS missing several pay periods. Obviously, the people that really suffer are not the administrators or the teachers but the students.

Although several factors including corruption and mismanagement contributed to the bankruptcy of the Detroit Public School System, the biggest factor was the rapid decreased in enrollment. Enrollment in some districts had decreased nearly 50% since 2001. Today, nearly 35% of all schools in Detroit are vacant. And since state funding for education is determined by enrollment, revenue has declined precipitously since 2001 as well. Although the school system had a surplus in 2001, the school was unable to pay all of its bills just seven years later.

The story of Salah James is important because it illustrates the current status quo in declining cities. *Unplanned shrinkage*, or the unintended effects of rapid population decline with correspondent declines of the economic base in an urban area, has been happening in older American cities for more than 40 years.

Since the 1960's, residents have fled these older American cities in pursuit of better living standards in the suburbs or better employment opportunities in the South and West. Whether we observe the older urban centers of Southeast Connecticut (Hartford, Bridgeport, and New Haven), the older urban centers of the mid-Atlantic (Baltimore and Philadelphia) or the numerous older urban centers of the Midwest (Youngstown, Flint, Detroit or Cleveland), unplanned shrinkage has had a disastrous impact on these cities. Increased poverty rates and unemployment rates are a direct result of unplanned shrinkage. Moreover, 16 of the 25 most dangerous cities in the United States in 2012 suffered from rapid population declines since the 1960's.

Urban planning has historically been associated with planning for the rational growth of the urban environment. Since the rampant urbanization of the United States is fairly recent and corresponds to the Great American Industrial Age that occurred around the start of the $20^{th}$ century, this association is logical. However, urban planners need to plan for the city given the current socio-economic realities that face it today. If the United States is indeed headed toward a decade of little or no job creation, why haven't cities, especially the oldest ones, begun planning for cities with a smaller economic base and a corresponding smaller population?

Planned shrinkage addresses this reality by rationally creating a smaller footprint for a city that inevitably has and will become smaller. What has occurred in Detroit, Baltimore, Flint(Michigan) or Youngstown(Ohio) has been "unplanned shrinkage," and as a result, these cities have become shells of their former selves. Formerly vibrant commercial corridors sit neglected and vacant. Although these cities have exhibited an overall population decline of 50%, many neighborhoods within these cities have lost 70% to 80% of their populations. That is astounding. Some residents of these cities live on blocks with many more vacant properties than occupied ones. Planned shrinkage attempts to address the realities of older America cities with a bloated infrastructure and a diminishing population and economic base. It also has the potential of reviving the economic base of the urban core and creating new employment opportunities for its residents.

forward thinking

## B.

**F**lint, Michigan was founded by Jacob Smith in 1819 originally as a fur trading outpost with active trading between Native Americans and Whites. By the turn of the century, lumber and carriage manufacturing supplanted fur trading.

The lumber and carriage manufacturing infrastructure in Flint made it a natural home for the young automobile industry. Buick Motor Company was founded in Flint, and William Durant moved to Flint in 1908 to found General Motors. Flint grew with the automobile industry. Major suppliers such as Delphi became headquartered in Flint.

By 1950, Flint had a population of 200,000. African-American and White families were able to live the American dream and enjoy an upwardly mobile, middle-class lifestyle based on increasing salaries and opportunities from the auto industries.

Besides the auto industry, Flint also benefitted substantially from the war effort during World War II. African-Americans from the South were drawn to the many manufacturing jobs in the city. The city slowly diversified. Today, the population of Flint is nearly divided between African-Americans and Whites.

But by the 1970's, the decline of the American auto industry had a disastrous impact on the city. With the closing of auto plants, residents left the city and communities became abandoned. The effect of this unplanned shrinkage was highlighted in the 1989 documentary "Roger and Me" by Michael Moore. By 2000, the population of the city had dropped to 88,000 or nearly 50% of its peaked population in the 1950's.

Flint today represents the most prominent national example of unplanned shrinkage. In 2014, the city switched the water supply from the Detroit Water System to the Flint river. Between 2014 and 2016, Flint planned to build a new water pipeline to Lake Huron. The usage of the Flint River was meant as a temporary measure to save the city money while the pipeline was built. Moreover, the city neglected to treat the water from the Flint River with an anti-corrosive agent. Without the proper treatment of the water, lead immediately began leaching from the aging water supply lines into homes.

Lead level spiked as soon as the water supply was switched.

Patrick Breysse, director of the CDC's National Center for Environmental Health, stated that "This crisis was entirely preventable, and a startling reminder of the critical need to eliminate all sources of lead from our children's environment". According to the Mayo Clinic, children under the age of 6 are particularly vulnerable because lead severly impacts a child's mental and physical development.

"We care about (lead) so much because it impacts your cognition and your behavior," said Dr. Hanna-Attisha, the doctor who first sounded the alarm about Flint's lead crisis. "It actually drops your IQ. Imagine what we've done to an entire population. We've shifted that IQ curve down. We've lost our high achievers, the next kid who's going to be neuro-surgeon, and we have all these children who may now need remedial services."

Today, the leaders of Flint are waging a battle over the future direction of the city. Dan Kildee, the former county treasurer, argues that a smaller city will be a more manage-able one. In a recent New York Times article, he argued:

> "What we really need is a new map, literally a design of the city that looks at every block in every neighborhood, and then makes deci-sions about where it makes sense to either let nature take the land back or to create some intentional open green space, so that 100,000 people can live in a city that does not look half-empty."

Recent new legislation from the Michigan legislature allows the counties to use tax foreclosures to capture vacant properties and to place those properties in a land bank.

Before the land bank, vacant properties either stayed in legal limbo for years or were purchased by speculators who warehoused vacant properties. The land bank allows the county to quickly seize vacant properties and coordinate development efforts. Vacant land could be used for green space, light industrial use, or other potential economic development activities.

Kildee said he hopes that the land bank will be the start of a smaller but greener and more efficient Flint.

> "If they choose to live where the population is essentially gone, we need to give them something green and beautiful. But give them the choice to relocate into a denser, more high-functioning neighborhood. That's really the point of all this: The people who live in these neighborhoods deserve better. We have to think about what's in their interest."

Opponents of Kildee's plan argue that choosing which neighborhoods to save or demolish is unfair to local residents. Mayor Dayne Walling, who was mayor in Flint during the water crisis, calls the whole "shrinking city" idea misguided and says it smacks of surrender.

"There are certainly thousands of properties that need to be demolished — they're not fit for human habitation," Walling acknowledges. "But it doesn't follow that the other residents on the block want to move to some other place."

Clearly Mayor Walling never heard of unplanned shrinkage or the disastrous impact declining cities have on its residents. He simply needs to ask any of the parents with young children impacted by the Flint water crisis how dangerous unplanned shrinkage can be.

C.

The benefits of planned shrinkage for declining cities are manifold. If the primary problem facing declining cities is a declining tax base and the delivery of basic services to an ever-needier population, planned shrinkage directly confronts these problems by lowering the cost of service delivery and potential allowing cities to lessen the tax burden on its citizens. Planned shrinkage achieves this by lessening the footprint of the city and creating a denser yet livable city.

Planned shrinkage traces its roots to the fiscal crisis in New York during the 1970's. Roger Starr, a prominent planner and bureaucrat, first discussed planned shrinkage as a way to combat the devastation occurring in the South Bronx during this time. A quote from an article he wrote in the *New York Times Magazine* in November, 1978 best describes his notion of planned shrinkage.

> "If the city is to survive with a smaller population, the population must be encouraged to concentrate itself in sections that remain alive. This sort of internal resettlement or the natural flow out of areas that have lost their general attraction must be encouraged…. Gradually, the city's population in

older sections will begin to achieve a new configuration, one consistent with a smaller population that has arranged itself at densities high enough to make the provisions of municipal services economical."

As the Housing Commissioner for New York City, Starr attempted to implement this policy in several parts of the South Bronx in the 1970's. Central to his thesis was the notion that vacant land could more easily achieve its highest and best use faster than land that was partially occupied for residential or commercial purposes. Vacant land also required fewer municipal services, and its eventual highest and best utilization could lead to an increased economic base for the city. He proposed turning many parts of the South Bronx into parks, and was successful in converting several residential blocks into light industrial facilities.

Although Starr's rationalization for planned shrinkage was sensible in the 1970's, the need for planned shrinkage in New York City was eliminated due to the renaissance that occurred in New York after 1990. Between 1990 and 2005, New York City added 1,500,000 new residents. Immigration increased the population of the city by nearly 20%. The city invested heavily in new housing development and embarked on one of America's most robust municipal new housing development programs.

Finally, New York's reemergence as a worldwide financial capital, combined with the factors previously mentioned, transformed many of New York's blighted neighborhoods. (This renaissance of New York in the 1990's will be discussed later in the book.)

Many municipalities have not been so fortunate since the 1970's. As shown previously, older Northeast and Midwestern cities such as Detroit, Baltimore, Philadelphia, New Haven, and Cleveland have continued to lose their populations during this time period. And unfortunately, these cities have also not been able to replace their manufacturing base with industries than can benefit from the globalization of our economy

Let's examine how planned shrinkage can work. In a hypothetical example, if a declining city has 10 major neighborhoods with an average vacancy rate of 25%, the city still needs to service all 10 neighborhoods with property tax revenues 25% below optimal levels. Let's assume that the city determines that the elimination of one neighborhood with a vacancy rate in excess of the average should be eliminated. Residents will be relocated to other neighborhoods with lower vacancy rates. The land in this neighborhood can be utilized for its highest and best use. In the future, the highest and best use may be determined to be green/recreational space, food production or light manufacturing or other commercial activities.

*not planned?* (handwritten margin note)

*The cost of basic service delivery in a municipality is as much dependent on the square footage of the city as it is on population size.* The maintenance of the city's sewer and road system is determined more by spatial size than population size. Even if a neighborhood is half vacant, the water delivery system and roads still need to be serviced as if they were fully utilized. Just ask the residents of Flint, Michigan the importance of a proper water delivery system.

The delivery of basic health and safety services also becomes more efficient with a smaller footprint. In the same hypothetical example mentioned above, the city may have allocated one police precinct and one fire station to every neighborhood in the city. Let's also assume that each precinct or station has 100 officers and 10 firemen. By eliminating one neighborhood and one corresponding precinct or station, the city can either choose to maintain basic health and safety services to its residents and lessen its overall costs for these services by 10%, or maintain those costs and increase service delivery by 10%. Either way, both choices would be preferable compared to the status quo, which is to minimize service delivery to all neighborhoods due to lower tax revenue. Since service delivery is typically lessened in poorer neighborhoods first, planned shrinkage would have the greatest impact on service delivery to the poorest residents.

The above example also applies to another major expense for cities – public education. In our hypothetical example, if every neighborhood has its own school district, the elimination of one neighborhood and one school district will allow the city to devote 10% more resources to every school. Although the remaining school districts will increase in size by 10%, the increased flexibility of allocating resources toward smaller classroom sizes, better after-school or arts programs, or increased capital expenditures on school buildings far outweighs the rational for keeping an underutilized school district open.

These are the long-term impacts of planned shrinkage. But the long-term can be very long. The short-term impacts of planned shrinkage should not be ignored. Opponents of planned shrinkage have correctly highlighted the increased short-term capital costs as a major obstacle towards the implementation of this policy. Going back to our hypothetical example, all residents will need to be relocated from the neighborhood slated for elimination. Homeowners will need to be compensated for the value of their properties. Infrastructure in this neighborhood such as community facilities, schools, precincts, or fire stations will need to be demolished or secured against vandalism. If the city can't afford the delivery of basic services for its current residents, how can the city afford to pay for these capital costs?

The federal government needs to assist cities in addressing these issues; it has a responsibility to assist cities. Many planners have argued that the federal government abandoned

Service Delivery

American cities in the 1970's and have continued that policy through today. Loic Wacquant in his book, *Urban Outcasts*, illustrates that the federal government during the Nixon administration had initiated planned shrinkage through eliminating successful policies from the Johnson's Administration War on Poverty. He writes:

> "At the federal level, after Nixon's landslide re-election in 1972, a sudden turnaround in urban policies was affected by the federal government that practically annulled and then reversed the modest gains of the War on Poverty."

Ronald Reagan continued the federal government's policy of underfunding urban initiatives by diminishing the budgets of agencies such as the Department of Housing and Urban Development (HUD) which was dedicated to assisting America's urban areas. During Reagan's tenure, the budget for HUD was cut from $74 billion to $19 billion.

The responsibility of the federal government in assisting declining cities is also of national importance. According to the report published by the United Nations on global urbanization in 2008, more than 81% of all Americans live in urban areas. At least 40% of these urban residents live in the Midwest or Northeast, and these areas have a high concentration of declining cities. Our analysis of the top 100 American cities demonstrated that 13 million Americans live in declining cities. American International Group (AIG) with only 106,000 employees has received more than $81 billion in federal bailout funds. Shouldn't America do the same for the 13 million residents in declining cities?

The contribution from the federal government to save a declining city would not be nearly as significant as its bailout of Wall Street. The contribution could be in the form of a loan instead of a grant. In the long run, this assistance would cost tax payers nothing. Financial models already exist that would allow the government to provide loan guarantees to municipalities that seek planned shrinkage as an alternative to further decline. The costs of the planned shrinkage mentioned above can be paid for by bond revenues backed by the federal government. The source of revenue to repay the bonds will stem from the potential future revenue from the uses of the land designated for planned shrinkage.

This form of financing infrastructure improvements through future tax revenue is called Tax incremental Financing and has been used in the United States since the 1950's.

In our hypothetical example, the city eliminates a sparsely populated residential neighborhood. Although the neighborhood was nearly 50% vacant, significant development of any sort could not occur because the vacant land was interspersed amongst occupied residential structures and community facilities. The costs for resident relocation, homeowner reimbursement, and demolition of infrastructure would be paid through bond revenues.

After planned shrinkage, the neighborhood can now achieve its highest and best use. The neighborhood may be repositioned as an urban farm that can provide food to the city in a more environmentally conscious way. The urban farm can provide employment opportunities to local residents and lessen the carbon footprint of the city by lessening truck hours to and from the city that transport food from more distant farms.

Another potential use could be recreational / green space for the city. A small entry fee could be charged for the use of the park or federal funds designated green space could now be used to maintain this new park. Larger scale light manufacturing facilities could be built on the new site. Other commercial activities such as bio-technical uses could also be implemented.

Any potential revenue generated from the future uses could be used to repay the federal bonds used for planned shrinkage. In our example, the capital costs of planned shrinkage would be zero for the city and zero for the federal government since their loan would be repaid by future tax revenue. Many cities already use a similar strategy for smaller scale development. For example, tax increment financing (TIF) has been utilized in California since 1952. California and Illinois lead the nation in the use of TIF districts.

Essentially, municipalities use tax increment financing to fund the capital costs of infrastructure improvements in certain districts. The municipality determines the initial tax base prior to the capital costs. The municipality then raises TIF bonds to pay for a new road, bridge, sewer system or other infrastructure improvement. The infrastructure investment from the TIF bonds will lead to development activities that will lead to a higher tax base in the district. The incremental increase in the tax base is used to pay the debt service on the TIF bonds.

Cities and the federal government can finance planned shrinkage utilizing many of the elements found in TIF projects. The federal government would guarantee any bonds issues by cities for planned shrinkage. The federal government will also supervise the implementation of planned shrinkage to ensure that all municipalities fairly award contracts and land to the highest bidder. Finally, the federal government will also document the successes and failures with the implementation of planned shrinkage in order to make improvements to the program. The federal government is a necessary component to implement planned shrinkage in municipalities throughout the Northeast and Midwest. Arguably, the abandonment by the federal government of urban America in the early 1970's led to the poor state of many urban areas.  By re-engaging the federal government in the problems of urban America, these problems confronting urban America can be fixed.  This re-engagement by the federal government may even create new economic opportunities for local residents.

D.

**C** ase Study – Youngstown, Ohio

> "By the late 1970's, the plan was without foun-
> dation and virtually obsolete. Youngstown
> lacked direction through its decline, and with-
> out vision languished for the next twenty-five
> years" (www.youngstown2010.com)

Youngstown was established in 1802 by John Young. Immigrants from Eastern Europe as well as German and Irish immigrants settled in Youngstown to take advantage of the coalmines in the Mahoning Valley. Youngstown became the commercial hub in the area and its connection to the Erie Canal in the early 19th century helped spur its growth. The aggregation of steel mills in Youngstown attracted African-Americans from the South in the early 20th century and helped transform the city into a more diverse community.

Youngstown was home to several large steel manu-facturers including the National Steel Company and the Youngstown Sheet and Tube Company. By 1950, Youngstown had grown to more than 200,000 residents. However, its economy was almost completely dependent on steel and was not diversified like larger Midwestern cities like Chicago, Cleveland or Pittsburgh. Youngstown thrived until the collapse of the steel industry in the 1970's.

The collapse of the steel industry was devastating for Youngstown. By 1979, Youngstown Steel was shut and larger manufacturers such as Republic Steel and U.S. Steel filed bankruptcy. During this time, the community lost 40,000 manufacturing jobs, nearly $500MM in net worth, and more than half of the tax revenue for school taxes.

Youngstown still has not recovered from the collapse of the steel industry in the 1970's. The population has shrunk from 200,000 in 1970 to 80,000 people in 2010. Large companies there with significant operations include General Motors, Schwebel Bakery, and Arby's. But the demise of the auto industry may spell further trouble for the city, as the economic base of the city remains industrial.

The city also has benefitted from two mayors who have confronted the economic malaise and reality of Youngstown directly. The previous mayor, George McKelvey, served two terms starting in 1998 and was the first mayor to openly embrace planned shrinkage as a viable plan for the city. Jay Williams was the first mayor elected as an independent since 1922 and also campaigned strongly for planned shrinkage for the city.

Youngstown has also benefitted from the two higher education facilities that are in the area, Youngstown State

University and Kent State University. The Shrinking Cities Institute is located at Kent State University and was founded in 2005 to address the problems facing Youngstown and other cities in Ohio. The institute worked with the city of Ohio to create the "Youngstown 2010" plan.

Youngstown 2010 was developed in 2002 by the city of Youngstown and Youngstown State University. Both institutions were embarking on a review of their Consolidated / Campus Plan and decided to join forces to create a plan that worked for both of them. Planners spent a substantial amount of time and met with numerous community leaders. The culminations of the community planning process were meetings that involved 14,000 residents, or one out of every six residents in the community.

Youngstown 2010 is driven by three fundamental principles:

1. Accepting that Youngstown is a smaller city;
2. Defining Youngstown role in the new regional economy; and
3. Improving Youngstown's image and enhancing its quality of life.

The first and second principals formed the crux of the fundamental changes the city intends to embark upon. The city leaders, through this plan, acknowledged that the urban infrastructure is oversized given the current and projected population for the city. Although Youngstown was the third largest steel manufacturer in the nation before 1950, the collapse of the steel manufacturing has forced the city to rethink its position and its chances for future economic development. Youngstown, probably more than most cities, has endured the negative results of unplanned shrinkage. Its population has decreased by nearly 60% in 40 years. The Youngstown 2010 Plan is an opportunity for the city to proactively plan for its future.

> "This process is nothing short of a paradigm shift. Former knee jerk reactions to events outside the city's control have failed. A proactive approach toward the future is the last chance for sustainability, perhaps even survival. To be proactive involves a clear vision of what the future can be and a road map towards that end.   This planning process involves both a vision and a plan that will give direction to Youngstown through 2010 and provides the foundation for a future beyond that point." (www.youngstown2010.com)

Youngstown leaders took great care to maximize community input. Hundreds of community volunteers were used to categorize every parcel of land in the city. Media, including the television network PBS as well as local newspapers, were used to advertise the progress of the plan to the residents. Between the unveiling of the vision statements in 2002 and the completion of the comprehensive plan in 2005, more than 5,000 residents participated in the creation of the plan.

The plan used population decline and various housing indices (supply, age, and value) as barometers for the need for planned shrinkage. Not only has the population decreased by 60% since 1950, but there also exists an excess supply of housing stock. The surplus of housing stock was determined by dividing the population by the average size of household and comparing this number to actual number of housing units. Another key barometer, housing stock age, showed that the excess supply of housing units came from older units and not from the development of new housing units. Youngstown has seen very little development since 1990. Ninety percent of all housing was built before 1950.

The Youngstown 2010 plan created 11 planning districts and defined neighborhoods that were 1) growing; 2) in transition; and 3) unsustainable. The three indices used to categorize neighborhoods were 1) tax delinquencies; 2) property disrepair; and 3) population density. Vibrant neighborhoods had low tax delinquencies, property in good shape and high population densities; unsustainable neighborhoods had high structural index problems – low population densities combined with high tax delinquencies and property disrepair. Neighborhoods in transition suffered from many of the same problems as unsustainable neighborhoods but had normal population densities. Three out of 11 neighborhoods were identified as unsustainable.

The primary tool for the implementation of the new plan is a new zoning ordinance. The zoning ordinance is driven by four goals:

1.  Increase the amount of space devoted to parks and recreation;
2.  Create industrial districts that will promote greener technologies;
3.  Create vibrant residential neighborhoods; and
4.  Create a vibrant urban core.

Residential zoned areas have been decreased by 30%. Commercially zoned areas have been relegated to major thoroughfares. The proposed decreases in residential and commercial areas are far less than the actual decrease in population or vacancy rates in existing commercial areas. However, the plan does leave room for the future growth of the city. New recreational and industrial districts have taken the place of former residential and commercial districts. The plan has created a new zoning classification called Industrial Green, which envisions future industrial uses far different from current heavy industrial uses. Development in industrially green-zoned areas must by non-polluting and encourage the preservation of open space.

Other tools offered by Youngstown for the implementation of the plan include a $50,000 incentive payment for homeowners that move out of unsustainable neighborhoods and the active demolition of vacant structures in unsustainable neighborhoods.

According to the Vindicator, a local Youngstown newspaper, the implementation of this 30-year plan has gotten off to a slow start. The recession has slowed the redevelopment efforts of Youngstown. Also, several problems have arisen with the incentive package. First, the package is offered to all residents in the city instead of residents in unsustainable neighborhoods. Second, no homeowner has yet taken the package. The city clearly does not have enough resources to pay any homeowner who wishes to move and should focus its resources on clearing unsustainable neighborhoods.

Youngstown also has run out of funds for the demolition of vacant structures. Funding from the federal stimulus package has helped; however, the number of vacant homes demolished in 2011 was half the number demolished in 2008.

Although any plan on this scale will have detractors and short-term problems, the plan is a proactive yet conservative approach for dealing with the obvious problems facing

Youngstown. The status quo is not sustainable and has led to a 20% population decline every decade. The corresponding effect of a bloated urban infrastructure and dwindling tax base threaten the city's survival. Youngstown 2010 will succeed[1]. The ultimate implementation will probably be different from the original plan. However, by engaging residents about the problems facing their city and by developing a proactive approach to address the problems of shrinkage, the plan has already succeeded.

---

[1]

E.

The decline of some older American cities is inevitable. Yet, these urban areas have been a place for increased economic opportunities. This statement is best illustrated by understanding the converse argument. The preference of the suburban / rural lifestyle with ample green space and healthier living conditions has been argued and idealized since Thomas Jefferson and Alexander Hamilton argued the optimal direction of growth for this country. Jefferson told James Madison:

> "I think our governments will remain virtuous for many centuries as long as they are chiefly agricultural; and this will be as long as there shall be vacant lands in any part of America. When they get plied upon one another in large cities, as in Europe, they will become corrupt as in Europe."

The pollution, crime and poverty of the urban environment have been well chronicled. Charles Dickens became famous by chronicling the negative elements of a rapidly growing 19th century London.

However, urbanization, first a Western concept, has now become a global phenomenon. Whether we consider the case of African-Americans leaving the rural South for northern urban centers in pursuit of better economic conditions in the mid-20th century or Chinese citizens flooding urban centers in China in pursuit of the same thing, cities have historically been places that attract residents due to the promise of better economic opportunities.

There are many ways to judge the success of a city. Arguably, the most important metric for its success should be the direct economic development opportunities it offers it people. A city should also be judged by its delivery of essential services. The quality of life for its residents is dependent upon it.

Through confronting the reality of an urban core with a smaller economic base and smaller population, planned shrinkage can create a new vision and new direction of older American cities. High taxes can be addressed by decreasing the infrastructure of the city. Health and safety professionals can more easily assist or protect residents in a denser city. Services at underutilized schools can be condensed to expand services at more populous schools. Sanitation services can more easily occur in a city with a smaller footprint.

Additionally, land in the urban core which is currently underutilized as mostly vacant residential properties can be repositioned as green space or space for future economic development. New residential areas can be planned as more communities with greater commercial activities and easier delivery of essential municipal services become a draw again.

So far, we've discussed the benefits of planned shrinkage and a possible way to pay for the short-term costs of implementing such policy. The implementation of planned shrinkage involves two more crucial components: 1) community notification and involvement; and 2) political will to enact legislation for such policies.

*Community Involvement*

Planned shrinkage will involve the taking of property, the closure of neighborhoods, and significant development for those neighborhoods that remain. These activities will undoubtedly cause disruption in the lives of residents in affected neighborhoods. Municipal and civic leaders need to intimately understand and then communicate the tradeoff between short-term sacrifice and long term gain that planned shrinkage involves.

A hallmark of the Youngstown planned shrinkage strategy was the level of community input and community outreach. The city's leaders correctly estimated that in order to make planned shrinkage plausible, the community would need confidence in the transparency of the process. So Youngstown used every form of media (Internet, public television, billboards, and newspapers) and two years of community outreach to reinforce the transparency and efficacy of the process. In fact, the marketing campaign by Youngstown received an American Planning Association (APA) award in 2006.

Community involvement is also crucial because it allows the community to help direct the path that planned shrinkage takes in their community. Planners and government officials need information from the community in order to guide their decisions. Done successfully, planned shrinkage will involve the displacement of entire communities and the redevelopment of other communities. Information such as family composition, average family incomes, and ethnicity can only be gleaned from the community itself. The ultimate plan for a municipality should be informed both from the top-down by planners and officials and from the bottom-up from the community.

Community involvement adds a level of transparency which is necessary for any significant government involvement in people's lives. As allegations of nefarious business interests and insider deals poison the process of implementing planned shrinkage, the most effective antidote will be aggressive and sustained community outreach. The Internet provides an effective tool to both inform the community and receive input from the community as planned shrinkage progresses. It also allows for a relatively transparent process.

*Political Will*

The implementation of planned shrinkage will involve years of development activity within a municipality. The reallocation of infrastructure, the taking and development of property, and the relocation of affected community residents could easily take a decade or more. The short sightedness of most municipal politicians who are only interested in their next term makes the sustainability of such a policy difficult.

Although planned shrinkage needs to be directed and guided by the local community, its implementation will need to be administered on the state or federal level. State or federal agencies will be able to view and administer planned shrinkage without regard for myopic views from a few residents within a municipality and without regard for short-term political calculations.

The current morass in New Orleans provides a good example of the inability of a local community to direct large-scale development within its own borders. Hurricane Katrina was a disaster that killed thousands and affected hundreds of thousands of people. The city of New Orleans lost half its population and incurred property damage in the billions. Although the response of the Bush Administration was slow, the federal government did provided capital and aggressive tax incentives to encourage rebuilding.

Although Katrina occurred in 2005, New Orleans is still several years away from implementing a comprehensive reconstruction plan for the city. Residents have been allowed to rebuild in flood prone areas. Disagreements amongst city officials have prevented a faster reconstruction effort. Crime and a lack of affordable housing remain persistent problems. The city has yet to create a comprehensive plan to guide the redevelopment efforts of the city.

Imagine the reconstruction effort if it was directed by the federal government or the State of Louisiana. Either institution could have used eminent domain to minimize new development in flood prone areas. Vacant parcels on higher ground could have been identified for high density, affordable housing to support the families displaced from flooded areas. Job training programs could have been established to allow local residents to take advantage of the economic development opportunities from the rebuilding effort. All new developments would be designed with green building principles.

Within 10 years after the flood, New Orleans could have a model American city and a showcase for modern building methods and planning policies. Instead, New Orleans remains mired in corruption and ineffective local politicians.

Other cities and towns contemplating planned shrinkage cannot make the same mistake. Although the plan needs to be created by the local municipality, the actual implementation should be administered by the State or Federal Government.

# THE NEW YORK CITY MIRACLE:

## How Immigration Saved New York City in the 1990'S

## A.

In the early 1970's, a young woman moved from El Salvador to New York City. She, like immigrants before and after her, came to New York to escape the crushing poverty of her homeland and make a better life for her and her family. She also left El Salvador to escape from her lying husband who thought that a wife's place was to be seen but not heard.

The young Central American woman settled in the Bronx with her child and quickly discovered a small Central American community. Her next-door neighbor was also from El Salvador and helped her to raise her little daughter. The young mother landed a job as a bookkeeper and took classes at night as an accountant. Her daughter excelled in school.

The lives of mother and daughter encountered many twists and turns. By the mid-1980's, the daughter was in high school. It was then that her mother, only in her mid-30's was diagnosed with breast cancer. She bravely fought the disease, but succumbed to the illness before her 40th birthday. The daughter was taken in by the next-door neighbor who raised her like her own. And, spared the indignity and uncertainty of foster care, the girl continued to excel in school.

Losing your mother in your teenage years is never easy. This is especially true for children of single mothers. However, the young daughter persevered. She graduated near the top of her class in high school, graduated from an Ivy League university and completed medical school. Today, Dr. Machuca is a physician in a small Bronx clinic helping impoverished Bronx residents get necessary health care. She could have practiced medicine anywhere and made heaps of money. Instead, she decided to return to her community and help other young mothers and daughters with their health care issues.

This story, although remarkable, highlights the incredible strength of immigrants to succeed against daunting odds. Most of us can recite similar immigrant stories within our own families, or at least in our communities.

The recent debate about immigration policy in the U.S. has devolved into a zero net gain contest. Opponents vehemently argue that immigrants are stealing American jobs, using taxpayer funds for social services, and diminishing the quality of life for American citizens. However, all of us know a Dr. Machuca. All of us intimately understand the courage and fortitude that our ancestors had when they left their home countries and came to this country in search of a better life. Unless you are Native American, we can all trace our lineage to a different country.

What if the debate about immigration policy could be elevated beyond a zero net gain conversation? What if immigration could be used as a tool to assist declining cities? As you have now learned from earlier chapters, the primary problem with declining cities is a declining economic base and declining population. The previous chapter discussed ways for declining cities to decrease their infrastructure in order to correctly accommodate their new, reduced size. A smaller infrastructure would lead to lower expenses for the city and allow for a better delivery of public services to the remaining residents. As the former mayor of Detroit, David Bing has said, "Detroit (formerly of a city of two million people) needs to learn to be the best 900,000 person city."

A pro-immigration strategy for certain declining cities may be useful for two reasons.

First, certain cities may not have the political will to encourage planned shrinkage. And second, some cities may need a pro-immigration strategy to promote growth once the infrastructure has been diminished to a sustainable size. It is no coincidence that some of these same declining cities were, in an earlier time, major hubs for immigrants. They were home to European immigrants and African-American immigrants from the South who sought to establish communities in these cities and seek better economic opportunities.

Today, immigrants are more likely to come from Latin America, Asia, and Africa, yet they are still coming to this country for the same reasons. The opponents of immigration would have our country take these hardworking, risk-taking

*domestic -*
*lack of hope*

individuals and leave them knocking on America's door. However, these immigrants, like immigrants before them, perfectly embody the American spirit of risk-taking and hard work. Why can't our national policy view these individuals as resources and direct them to our embattled declining cities? If these immigrants then create new businesses or new industries, it would help replenish the two very things leading to the decline: the population and the economic base.

As a planner and developer, I am an eternal optimist. And whether such a policy would actually work is indeed questionable. However, a pro-immigration policy like I have described – one that spurs economic growth and population increases – does have precedent.

In the 1990's, the growth of New York City was tremendously impacted by pro-immigration policies. Some would argue that the transformation of New York City from a declining city in the 1980's to a leading global city of the 21st century is a direct result of a pro-immigration policy. This chapter explores how immigration transformed New York City during the 1990's.

## B.

*The Rebirth of New York during the 1990's*

New York City's most famous neighborhood is Time Square. Times Square, a neighborhood once known for prostitutes and X-rated movie theatres, is now home to the finest Broadway theatres. And several new office buildings have been built in the area in recent years. A neighborhood once populated by homeless teenagers is now a tourist mecca for the world.

Times Square is not the only obvious change in New York City. Many neighborhoods that were considered "fringe" or "dangerous" in the 1980's are now thriving neighborhoods for the young urban professional. Harlem was transformed from an example of urban decay to an example of urban renaissance. Several malls were built along its main thoroughfare, West 125th Street; while many national tenants such as the Disney Stores, Old Navy, HMV, and Marshalls are now located in Harlem. Homes that were abandoned or used as crack houses a decade earlier now sell for more than a million dollars.

The New York miracle of rampant gentrification was not confined to Manhattan. Astoria in Queens and Fort Green in Brooklyn are two formerly working-class neighborhoods that were transformed into middle-class enclaves. Home prices have soared and retail options have increased.

Major economic and social indices show vast improvement in the city during the 1990's. According to the Disaster Center, major crime has dropped by 50% since 1993 and is at its lowest point since 1966. Per capita income increased from $21,902 to $38,045 or 73% from 1990 to 2000. Two hundred thousand additional units of housing were created, too.

*What led to this dramatic change in the 90's?* New York experienced a major immigration boom during the 1990's. Almost eight million new immigrants entered the country during this decade. Although the beginning of the 20th century is typically romanticized as the period of highest immigration in America, more immigrants entered the country between 1980 and 2000 than in any 20-year period in our history.

More importantly, 20% of all immigrants who entered the country during the 1990's came to New York City or Los Angeles. Between 1990 and 2000, New York City added 1,000,000 net new persons. Since 500,000 native New Yorkers left New York during this period New York actually added 1,500,000 new persons.

Immigration indeed altered New York City for the better. In 1989, New York was a declining large city with increasing crime and poverty rates. Poorer communities in New York, such as the South Bronx, Harlem, and Brownsville were condemned by social pundits to be in a permanent state of social and economic decline. Residential properties in these neighborhoods were nearly worthless. Between 1960 and 1990, New York City lost nearly 1,000,000 residents. Due to tax foreclosures and abandonment, the City of New York, itself, became the largest landlord in many of these communities.

The effect of immigration can be felt in all five boroughs. Neighborhoods such as Jackson Heights, Washington Heights, Central Harlem, and Bensonhurst have seen an influx of Central Americans, Dominicans, francophone West Africans and Russians, respectively. English is the second language in many of these neighborhoods. Since 1990, New Yorkers elected its first Asian Comptroller, first Native-born Jamaican Councilwoman, and several Dominican Councilpersons and State representatives. As of 2012, there are more people of color serving in the New York City Council than non-Hispanic Whites.

I have had my own real estate development company for 15 years. Luckily, we have never had an unsuccessful project. The quality of my business would be hampered without the large pool of very qualified immigrants that exist in New York City. My comptroller is a native of China who received her MBA at the University of Texas. When she first started working for me, her English was, at best, rough. One year later, she was completely fluent. Several of our construction managers were trained in the Dominican Republic as architects. My project manager was an officer in the military in Singapore who received his Master's Degree in Real Estate in New York City; and my senior project manager is a native of Columbia who has developed properties in Latin America. The perspectives of my employees are diverse and in many ways unique. Their points of view allow our firm to tackle difficult development problems from multiple perspectives. Diversity allows for a truly meritocratic work environment.

Stated differently, immigration increases the quality of the workforce that employers can choose from. America is the leading economic force in the world because it promotes and encourages the growth and creation of businesses. Immigration encourages the growth of business because it allows employers a tap the best and brightest employees in the World. This was true at the turn of the 20th century during the Second Industrial Revolution and remains true at the turn of the 21st century.

Anecdotal information about the benefits of immigration makes for great stories. However, theories can only truly be proven through qualitative analysis. Let's look at the data.

## C.

Let's compare several economic indices of census tracts with large immigrant populations and those with smaller immigrant populations in New York City. By focusing my analysis on New York City, external economic events that can cause increased economic growth have been isolated. Any macro event such as 9/11 or the economic bubble and subsequent decline of Wall Street would have a similar effect to neighboring households in New York City. Households in neighboring census tracts benefit equally from socioeconomic events that impacted New York during the 1990's. Therefore, differences in various economic indices should only be explained by differences in immigrant populations.

*Selected community boards*

Tables 1-4 illustrate a comparison of socio-economic data for representative community boards in Manhattan, the Bronx, Brooklyn and Queens utilizing 1990 and 2000 census data. Community boards are defined political entities in New York City which roughly encompass 1 or 2 neighborhoods. The community boards chosen represent working-class neighborhoods. The per capita and household incomes are below the average for New York City except for Queens. Therefore, socio-economic differences between working-class native households and working-class foreign households are not based on inheritance or other wealth transfers which may occur in middle-class or wealthy, native households. The community boards and neighborhoods that were chosen for this analysis are as follows:

| BOROUGH | COMMUNITY BOARD | NEIGHBORHOODS |
|---------|-----------------|---------------|
| Manhattan | 10 | Central Harlem |
| Manhattan | 11 | East Harlem |
| Bronx | 3 | Morrisania |
| Bronx | 6 | East Tremont |
| Brooklyn | 16B | Oceanville / Brownsville |
| Brooklyn | 4 | Bushwick |
| Queens | 12 | Jamaica |
| Queens | 13 | Queens Village |

Census tracts in Community Boards were divided by above average percentage of foreign-born residents ("High Foreign") and below average percentage of foreign born residents ("High Native"). I used the average percentage of foreign-born residents in the community board as the benchmark for determining High Foreign or High Native census tracts.

*Median Household Income*

Across New York City, High Foreign census tracts had a higher median income than High Native census tracts. The average difference was approximately 20%.

## Table 1- Differences in median income between High Native and High Foreign households

| HOUSEHOLD INCOME | | | | |
|---|---|---|---|---|
| Community Boards | Average | HIGH Foreign-Born | HIGH Native-Born | % Difference Foreign vs. Native |
| **Manhattan** | | | | |
| CB 11 (East Harlem) | 21,383 | 26,812 | 17,117 | 36% |
| CB 10 (Central Harlem) | 20,145 | 22,070 | 18,673 | 15% |
| **Bronx** | | | | |
| CB 3 (Morrisania) | 17,079 | 18,214 | 15,945 | 12% |
| CB 6 (East Tremont) | 17,877 | 20,832 | 15,661 | 25% |
| **Brooklyn** | | | | |
| CB 4 (Bushwick) | 22,103 | 23,391 | 21,056 | 10% |
| CB 16 (Brownsville) | 22,329 | 28,263 | 18,582 | 34% |
| **Queens** | | | | |
| CB 12 (Jamaica) | 43,801 | 43,283 | 44,087 | -2% |
| CB 13 (Queens Village) | 56,852 | 57,332 | 56,469 | 2% |

The most dramatic differences between High Native census tracts and High Foreign born tracts are in East Harlem and Bushwick. Both neighborhoods have experienced a dramatic increase in immigrant Latino households. In East Harlem, newly arrived Mexican immigrants have changed this traditionally Puerto Rican and African-American enclave. In Bushwick, Dominican and Central American households have been the most recent arrivals.

*Poverty Rate*

The average difference in poverty levels between High Foreign census tracts and High Native census tracts is 15%. These findings are consistent with the evidence about household income.

## Table 2 - Poverty rates between High Native and High Foreign households

| POVERTY RATES | | | | |
|---|---|---|---|---|
| *Community Boards* | *Average* | *HIGH Foreign-Born* | *HIGH Native-Born* | *% Difference Foreign vs. Native* |
| **Manhattan** | | | | |
| CB 11 (East Harlem) | 32.96 | 29.89 | 35.55 | -19% |
| CB 10 (Central Harlem) | 33.60 | 31.41 | 35.28 | -12% |
| **Bronx** | | | | |
| CB 3 (Morrisania) | 44.58 | 42.69 | 46.46 | -9% |
| CB 6 (East Tremont) | 41.10 | 39.10 | 42.59 | -9% |
| **Brooklyn** | | | | |
| CB 4 (Bushwick) | 34.76 | 34.98 | 40.59 | -12% |
| CB 16 (Brownsville) | 35.78 | 26.91 | 41.38 | -54% |
| **Queens** | | | | |
| CB 12 (Jamaica) | 13.71 | 13.53 | 13.81 | -2% |
| CB 13 (Queens Village) | 5.90 | 6.13 | 5.71 | 7% |
| Rates are out of 100 households. | | | | |

Immigrants did not come to America to be poor and left their home countries to avoid poverty. This motivation, or push factor, may explain the success that immigrants have in finding employment and earning a decent living even when living side-by-side with low-income, native-born families. The negative externalities of poor neighborhoods that may hinder working-class, native households are less of a hindrance to working-class, immigrant households. In other words, foreign households show a greater ability to avoid distractions like crime and drugs in low-income neighborhoods, which get in the way of native-born household's succeeding.

A second key reason for High Foreign census tracts having lower household poverty rates is recent immigrants' tendency to live "doubled-up" in their households. Households with more working adults will naturally have a lower rate of poverty.

The differences in poverty rates were especially dramatic in Manhattan CB – 11 (East Harlem) and Brooklyn CB -16 (Brownsville). Mexicans and West Indians are the most recent immigrants in these neighborhoods.

*Unemployment Levels*

Of the eight community boards analyzed for this study, all eight exhibited lower or equal unemployment rates for High Foreign census tracts as compared to High Native census tracts. The common myth of the new immigrant sitting at home taking advantage of various American welfare programs is debunked by these findings. George Borjas, a professor at the Harvard Kennedy School, describes the positive economic benefits of immigration in his paper "Immigration Policy and the American Economy."

## Table 3- Unemployment rates between High Native and High Foreign households

| UNEMPLOYMENT RATES | | | | |
|---|---|---|---|---|
| Community Boards | Average | HIGH Foreign-Born | HIGH Native-Born | % Difference Foreign vs. Native |
| **Manhattan** | | | | |
| CB 11 (East Harlem) | 18.31 | 14.72 | 21.13 | -44% |
| CB 10 (Central Harlem) | 18.40 | 18.32 | 18.46 | -1% |
| **Bronx** | | | | |
| CB 3 (Morrisania) | 22.25 | 22.06 | 22.45 | -2% |
| CB 6 (East Tremont) | 20.91 | 20.13 | 21.51 | -7% |
| **Brooklyn** | | | | |
| CB 4 (Bushwick) | 17.29 | 14.48 | 19.57 | -35% |
| CB 16 (Brownsville) | 20.23 | 15.42 | 23.27 | -51% |
| **Queens** | | | | |
| CB 12 (Jamaica) | 11.62 | 10.00 | 12.52 | -25% |
| CB 13 (Queens Village) | 7.45 | 6.74 | 8.02 | -19% |
| Rates are out of 100 households. | | | | |

The lower unemployment rates correspond with the increased higher participation in the labor force demonstrated by households in High Foreign census tracts. The lower unemployment levels of High Foreign census tracts also illustrates that an influx of immigrants can assist in the economic revitalization of a community since immigrants are more willing to take those jobs not desired by "native" Americans. In other words, immigrants provide a cheaper labor force for entrepreneurs and small business than native households or persons.

The most dramatic differences are in Manhattan CB-11 (East Harlem) and Brooklyn CB – 4 (Bushwick) and Brooklyn CB -16 (Brownsville). Mexicans, Dominicans, and British West Indians are the recent immigrants in these neighborhoods, respectively.

## D.

**M**uch has been written about the positive qualitative attributes of immigrants. More importantly, a great deal of xenophobic literature has described the negative socio- economic drain that immigration causes to our society. The quantitative data presented above about New York City paints a different picture. Immigrants helped to transform a city that nearly filed bankruptcy in the late 1970's into one of the most dynamic global cities in the world.

Immigrants are more likely to accept low wage, menial jobs than are native residents. Industries from home care to construction to agriculture would face sharply higher labor costs if they denied immigrant workers. These higher labor costs would either be borne by consumers in the form of higher prices or borne by small business owners through smaller profit margins. Consequently, lower labor costs are a competitive advantage to those communities that have a high influx of immigration.

Immigrants also introduce new foods, music, and other cultural markers to our society. The rich diversity of cities like New York, San Francisco and Miami are a direct result of their receptivity to immigrants.

Finally, immigrant households tend to be younger than native-born households. Given the aging of our population and diminishing native-born household size, immigrants keep our culture and workforce young and vibrant. The continued arrival of immigrants within our major ports of entry will, in all likelihood, continue for the foreseeable future. Cities, such as New York, Miami, San Francisco, and Los Angeles, have been forever influenced by old and new immigrants; and have clearly benefited from recent immigration through above average economic growth.

Previous economic cycles, such as those that occurred during the 1980's, positively affected the main commercial hubs of the city and upper middle-class residential neighborhoods while having very little impact on the city's poorer and blighted neighborhoods. The difference in the economic revival experienced during the 1990's and during other periods was the steep increase in population that occurred during this period. Since New York actually lost 500,000 native residents while gaining 1,500,000 immigrants, the credit for the population increase in New York and the corresponding improvements seen in formerly blighted neighborhoods such as Harlem, the South Bronx, and Brownsville must be attributed to these new immigrant populations.

If the support of immigration helped New York City, could it also help smaller declining cities? If so, how would a pro-immigration policy work? How do we get immigrants to create homes and communities in declining cities?

Although the immigration laws of the United States are changing, most variations of proposed changes involve tighter controls on new immigrants and the possible repatriation of current illegal immigrants. Today, we grant a certain number of visas to every country. Once a country exhausts their visa allocation, no further residents of that country can enter the United States for that year. Foreigners who long to come here can only do so illegally, using a variety of methods, often dangerous and including overstaying temporary education, work, or tourist visas.

Countries, especially those that routinely exhaust their allocation of annual visas, could be granted additional temporary visas for those individuals who agreed to relocate to cities that Americans have all but abandoned. The temporary visas would be for a period of two to five years. Upon the expiration of the temporary visa, the immigrant could apply for permanent status. However, the immigrant would need to prove their sustainability in this country through proof of employment or educational achievement.

This system of allotting temporary visas to those immigrants that agreed to set up shop in declining cities would encourage several positive outcomes. First, these immigrants, knowing that their visas are temporary, would work especially hard in their new communities to generate income for their families back home and for savings. They would also work hard in order to prove their sustainability in the United

States and increase their chances of attaining permanent residency.

As a result, our most failing cities would receive a new, fresh crop of young, hardworking, and aggressive employees. *And*, businesses in these cities would have a new source of clients and customers.

There is already precedent for this type of temporary visa system. Our current immigration system grants several ways to obtain temporary visas into the United States. Rural farmworkers are granted temporary visas to help farmers in the West and the South. The subculture of Mexican farm workers who obtain temporary visas to work on Californian farms is well documented. Without this form of reliable yet cheap labor, California farms would be uncompetitive. Philip Martin, a professor at UC Davis, describes the competitive disadvantage farms in California would face without immigrant workers in his paper "California's Farm Labor Market, the Case of Raisin Grapes."

The United States also grants temporary visas for technical workers and nurses. Health care and technology continue to be high growth industries in America. Foreign employees with temporary HI-B or HI-C visas provide a necessary source of labor for these industries. Farmers, health care and technology professionals have advocated hard for the continuation of these temporary visa programs in order to maintain their competitive edge.

Immigration indeed transformed New York City. The growth of industries like construction, health care, and technology have replaced the city's reliance on manufacturing, and that has been spurred by the steady flow of immigrants over the last 20 years. These immigrants then transformed decaying neighborhoods and were new customers for other consumer related businesses. "Fringe" neighborhoods with excess housing inventory became home to these new immigrant groups. With an influx of more than 1,000,000 immigrants since 1990, entire neighborhoods in New York City were transformed in order to create new housing for these households.

Why can't this be repeated across America? These cities are not commercial hubs like New York. But they do have businesses that could benefit from a temporary immigrant program that focused immigration into cities with declining populations and declining economic bases. The arrival of these immigrants would also stimulate new housing creation and introduce new customers to consumer related businesses.

# CONCLUSION

## A.

*The Fiscal Cliff* comes from the myriad of frustrating conversations I've had around the problems confronting many urban residents and many municipalities. While completing my master's degree in urban planning in New York City, I asked nearly all of my professors about the central problems facing challenging urban neighborhoods and poor urban residents. They all could describe how poverty, unemployment, a poor public education system, and substandard public education systems have had disastrous effects on poor urban residents. But that was as far as they could take the conversation.

Through extensive studies of various characters in the urban environment including students, the elderly, poor teenage mothers, and other characters that bear the brunt of these urban ailments, many academics have measured how these ailments impact these characters and how their impacts have changed over time. But, in my experience, they were far less effective in systematically approaching these various problems and putting forth possible solutions that could realistically solve these problems.

As a developer in the Northeast, I've talked to many municipal bureaucrats, urban planners, housing commissioners, and even some mayors about how these same problems impact their communities. Unlike academics, these individuals are on the front lines of solving these ailments. I have great respect for these practitioners. They work long hours for government pay to coordinate services for urban residents. They forsake more lucrative careers in private industry in order to "give back," "help others," and "make a difference."

Before Shaun Donovan became President Obama's housing czar and Secretary of the Department of Housing and Urban Development, he was the housing commissioner for New York City. While he was in this position, I met Shaun a few times and even hosted a reception for him and the African-American real estate community in New York City. Donovan, a graduate of Harvard University, is not only an extremely bright and capable individual, but he also has in-depth knowledge about housing development. He could easily have a very successful career in real estate finance or development. However, he has chosen to help our nation and command an often criticized government agency.

Bureaucrats like Donovan spend an incredible amount of time working within their organizations to study and address urban ailments that impact urban residents. However, they are so busy promoting programs that address these problems that they cannot ask the bigger questions like, where do these problems come from and how can they be permanently addressed? They unfortunately are surrounded by trees and often cannot look at the forest in front of them. They are doctors in the emergency room with too many patients. They spend all of their time addressing symptoms and not enough time asking about the underlying problems that cause the symptoms.

In other words, these urban ailments of poverty, unemployment, substandard education and substandard health care are not problems but *symptoms*. I purposely have called them symptoms to demonstrate the point that these conditions only provide insight into deeper problems that impact urban communities.  Although these symptoms also manifest themselves in vibrant and healthy cities, the manifestation of these symptoms in declining cities come from the failure to address issues of bloated infrastructure, higher tax bases, declining populations and weakening economic potential.

As an affordable housing real estate developer, my profession involves solving large problems. Our clients include municipalities, community organizations, and financial institutions that seek to build affordable housing in poor communities.  We also work with many vendors such as architects, builders, attorneys, and engineers to solve a large problem and execute the solution of that problem. The manifestation of the solution is a new or renovated building that provides descent housing for poor residents.  The problem is how to provide new housing at an affordable level to this population. The problem may also involve attracting capital to a project or devising a building that addresses the engineering difficulties inherent in any new site.

Although I, along with my staff, spend a great deal of time managing vendors and marshaling resources in order to build a new affordable housing development, all of this effort is meaningless without a keen understanding of the problem. I've worked with some of the best architects and builders in New York City. However, an unknown environmental issue can scuttle the best development plans.

I also work with some leading financial institutions in New York City. Even during the financial crisis of 2008, these firms helped us raise nearly $100MM in debt and equity capital to build several developments that provided housing for more than 300 families. However, we also spent a great deal of time talking to local community politicians and stakeholders in order to understand what type of development they wanted. Without buy-in from the local community, our ability to raise capital for a new development becomes irrelevant. In other words, without an understanding of the nature of a particular problem, our firm's ability as experienced developers becomes irrelevant. We would end up with structurally deficient buildings or buildings without any community support. We spend a great deal of time in our office trying to understand the problems that any particular new development may pose before attempting to corral resources and create a solution.

Unfortunately, I have not always proposed the right solution to a problem. In 2005, when my firm opened a second office in Baltimore, we were confident in our ability to raise capital and attract competent vendors who understood how to build affordable housing. There were many potential sites suitable for new development. However, we did a poor job of understanding the local community. We proposed housing that was out of scale with the local community. After 18 months of trying to convince the community of our proposal, we abandoned our development and shut down our office.

I will not pretend that the solutions put forth in *The Fiscal Cliff* address all the symptoms that confront many urban municipalities or that they are absolutely the right solutions. I'm hopeful that the ideas put forth here of planned shrinkage and planned immigration can assist cities in fixing their problems. Other municipalities may propose derivatives of these solutions, which are better suited for their specific location. I am confident that the problems can be solved.

I am also confident that stakeholders, planners, and academia need to ask the right questions in order to obtain the right answers. The symptoms of poverty, crime, poor health care and poor education seem intractable because stakeholders have asked the wrong questions.

Municipal leaders in fast growing or vibrant cities could meaningfully address these symptoms by allocating greater resources to them. Their unwillingness to do so may stem from other needs or priorities that leaders have for their cities. Municipal leaders in declining cities are unable to address these ailments because they lack the resources to do so. Address the declination of population and economic base within these cities and these symptoms will be diminished.

The twin storm of declining residential populations and declining economic base erodes the very core of a city. More importantly, it diminishes the rationale for a city's existence in the first place. People come and stay in cities for jobs. If jobs leave and are not replaced, people will follow. As people follow, more economic displacement occurs which leads to a further depopulation of a city.

These twin problems lead to the myriad of issues exhibited by declining cities. They are unable to provide basic public safety to all corners of a community because of the many vacant housing and community structures. Public safety is a large part of any municipal budget. With cities and states facing large budget deficits during this recession, municipalities are forced to cut this basic service to balance their budgets.

East St. Louis is a near suburb of St. Louis and is a part of the Greater St. Louis metropolitan area. The deindustrialization of the St. Louis area had already severely impacted East St. Louis before the Great Recession. The city had experienced population loss of more than 50% from its peak in the 1950's. The Great Recession has caused even more damage to this city. In order to balance the budget, the mayor has proposed cutting one-third of the police force. Today, the city has a force of only 100 officers. Reverend Joseph Tracy, a prominent local pastor, told residents at a local community meeting "It's an open field day now…the criminals are going to run wild."

As someone that grew up during the crack epidemic in Harlem during the 1980's and someone that visited East St. Louis during my trips cross-country, the thought of a diminished police force there is alarming. East St. Louis is well known as an example of urban blight and is arguably one of the most dangerous parts of St. Louis.   These cuts will leave only one patrolman for the midnight shift for the entire community. Pastor Joseph got it right unfortunately. Criminals will run wild.

The twin problem of a declining economic base and declining population also causes municipalities to lower their expenditures on public education.  In 2012, six in every 10 teenagers that attended a Cleveland high school did not graduate.  The City of Cleveland has the third highest dropout rate in the country.

Cleveland, due to the previous budget cuts caused by a diminishing tax base and the Great Recession, is now selling 25 of their public school structures.  With approximately 125 buildings, Cleveland is selling or demolishing 20% of their public schools. Through the sale of these buildings, city leaders hope to raise sorely needed funds or to diminish their expenditures on vacant buildings.

Obviously, Cleveland could use more resources and a different strategy to educate its children. The current recession has forced many recent college graduates to take menial jobs because of the persistency of high unemployment in the United States. High school graduates have fared worse. A high school dropout in Cleveland, which describes 60% of its students, has a low probability of success. Cleveland should be debating various educational initiatives and corresponding increases in resources to educate its children. The demolition of public school structures is probably not one of the ways to improve test scores or graduation rates.

The possible solutions proposed in *The Fiscal Cliff* require massive resource reallocation and dramatic policy shifts. Many may argue that the current situation within declining or depressed American cities does not warrant such drastic changes. The status quo, or marginal changes to the current status quo, would cause less dislocation and is more achievable than solutions proposed in this book.

Can the status quo be maintained? Can declining American cities address their situations without significant changes to policy and a significant reallocation of resources?

## B. The risk of the status quo

The Great Recession has exposed the dichotomy between growing and declining American cities. Our analysis indicates that more than 20% of all large American cities are declining. These cities are disproportionately concentrated in the Northeast and the Midwest. Both areas have been hit hard by a gradual shift in the American economy from industrial to service industries and have been hard hit by the rapid increase in unemployment caused by the Great Recession.

Two states that have been hit particularly hard by the Great Recession are Ohio and Michigan. Detroit is routinely referred to as the classic example of an industrial Midwestern city in decline. Detroit, though, is just a proxy for many cities in Ohio and Michigan that are in decline. Flint, Michigan and Youngstown, Ohio are obviously in decline. How will they be impacted by the Great Recession?

The effects of the Great Recession on Detroit are already obvious. The official unemployment rate in Detroit is 27% or more than one in four adults looking for work cannot find a job. According to the Huffington Post if we include adults who are discouraged and have given up looking for work, the actual unemployment rate in Detroit is nearly 50%.

So how does an effective unemployment rate of 50% affect a city? The median real estate sales price in 2010 was $18,000 and nearly the same price that one could purchase a home for in Detroit in 1960. In October of 2009, the city auctioned nearly 9,000 homes. Only 1,800 homes received any bid, and the average bid price was $1,500. In other words, homes in certain neighborhoods in Detroit are now worthless and cannot even be given away. As this book goes to print, Detroit has filed bankruptcy and residents continue to wonder what will happen with their city once the filing is complete.

This has become the status quo in many declining American cities. Homes built in a different time for a soaring population which was employed at the local plants or factories are now worthless. Many cities, such as Cleveland, try to dispose of excess infrastructure like schools in a misguided attempt to augment declining tax revenue.

The American free market economic system is ideal for a growing economy. Easy access to capital markets, lightly regulated markets, and low taxes allow businesses to flourish. At the beginning of the 20th century, Detroit was a growing city with a new, dynamic and young auto industry that propelled growth. Auto manufacturers and suppliers were able to start businesses without much interference from government rules or regulators. Access to capital markets allowed these businesses to grow and hire people. Developers, observing the industrial growth in the city, built homes throughout the city to address this growing population. The population of Detroit grew from 300,000 to 1,500,000 people between 1930 and 1960. In this same 30-year period, developers create more than 400,000 units of housing for this population.

A city needs more than factories and housing. With a growing tax base, Detroit was able to create infrastructure such as schools and hospitals to service its new residents. Many schools and hospitals were built during this period. The Detroit Institute for the Art, the leading art institute in the city, was built in 1927. The American system of capitalism, lightly regulated markets, open access to capital and graduated taxes on income allowed for the growth of Detroit.

But this same system is less able to create solutions or mechanisms to assist declining cities. Today, Detroit has thousands of houses abandoned by former residents or former employees of its many auto-manufacturing plants. The city has been forced to shutter old schools and hospitals that have low demand and were supported by diminishing taxes. How does the city plan for diminishing resources and continue to optimize the delivery of basic services to its residents?

Capitalism's response to this vexing problem is awkward, at best. Individual homeowners make the decision to abandon their homes based on their particular needs. The search for a job or a better valued home in a different neighborhood may convince the homeowner that abandonment is the best course of action. Other homeowners on the same block may decide to remain due to their job or familial situation. Although certain neighborhoods in Detroit and other failing Midwestern cities are 30% to 50% vacant, the vacant land is difficult to use because it is so randomly scattered throughout a block instead of adjacent to each other or contiguous.

Real estate appraisers use the concept of "highest and best use" to determine the maximum value of basic land based on the highest and best use of the land by a potential user. In other words, the highest and best use for a vacant lot with great access to the highway may be commercial or light industrial while the highest and best use for vacant land with access to all utilities and nearby a school maybe residential.

Capitalism and the corresponding lack of regulations and limited role of government in planning projects allows two homeowners on the same block to make very different decisions about abandoning or remaining in their home. The actions of these homeowners, guided by the invisible hand of capitalism, yields vacant parcels of land mixed between occupied homes and buildings. On a dilapidated block in Detroit, there may be 20,000 square feet of land on the block interspersed with another 20,000 square of land occupied by residents. The vacant land on this block may be found in 2,000 and 3,000 square foot lots throughout the block. However, these lots are much less desirable to a potential user than one contiguous 20,000 square foot parcel. Whereas a developer could plan a small subdivision on 20,000 square feet or a small retail operator could locate their business on this land or an urban farm could utilize the land to grow specialty vegetables for the surrounding neighborhood, the utilization of scattered lots of 2,000 to 3,000 square feet is best used just for a small house.

In this example, capitalism doesn't extract maximum value from this vacant parcel; it minimizes the potential uses of this vacant land and minimizes the value. Imagine if the city planned for the decrease in populations in their municipalities. The city could survey blocks for vacancy rates in excess of 50%. It could then incentivize people living on these blocks to relocate to more densely populated areas. Once blocks were made entirely vacant, it could reposition this land for its highest and best use. The incentives for relocation could be paid for by the decreased time vacant property would be off line and off the city's tax rolls. Instead of 20,000 of interspersed small vacant parcels, the city could market the same land that is now contiguous as an urban farm, light manufacturing facility or a more dense residential development.

Capitalism's response to declining cities is also awkward in other ways. Capitalism does not, at all, address the delivery of public services. The current American system of graduated taxation on income allows for cities to afford more services as its tax base expands. Our taxation system or economic system does not address the reallocation of scarce resources to better maximize the delivery of public goods to the population. Put differently, cities shutter schools and hospitals when they financially become unsustainable. This may result in residents in one neighborhood having significantly higher transit times to the nearest hospital because the hospitals in their neighborhood were shuttered due to financial troubles. A decision to close these facilities should instead be based on the most advantageous method of delivery of these important public goods such as public safety and health.

Detroit and many other older Midwestern and Northeastern cities are littered with vacant schools, hospitals and homes. The example of Cleveland selling 20% of their public school infrastructure is common amongst these cities. Wouldn't Cleveland be far wiser to close schools and hospitals in sparsely populated neighborhoods instead of denser ones? Wouldn't Cleveland also be wise to relocate people in sparsely populated neighborhoods to those neighborhoods that have a better ability to deliver public safety and public health more efficiently?

The status quo in declining cities already has high degree of abandoned infrastructure – homes, hospitals and schools. Free markets and small businesses have no way of redirecting the scarce resources of municipalities to assist more people. Only governments, with their powers of eminent domain and larger budgets, can perform this function. The invisible hand of capitalism is not enough to turn these cities around. We need more than an invisible hand. We need two hands, both legs and a strong back to help these cities.

In short, capitalism provides the necessary incentives for growth but is ill suited to plan for cities in decline. The maintenance of the public good or items such as public health, public safety and education is a by-product of capitalistic initiatives. Businessmen see the need for these items to better enhance their customer base and increase demands for their products. Better schools or enhanced public safety encourage families to move to a community. An increase in families increases demand for many consumer goods and is a benefit to retail stores. The business community works in tandem with government to promote the public good.

Once a city enters a period of decline, the business community struggles for its own survival. The public good becomes secondary to the maintenance of profit. Businesses are less apt to donate to worthy causes or community institutions. Since commercial revenue decreases, tax revenue from the business decreases. Certain businesses may even decide to leave the city altogether. In periods of decline, the business community conspires against the government to promote the public good.

Cities need to rely on a different system to plan for itself in periods of decline. Cities need to engage in long term planning based on the long-term needs of its constituents. Resources should be allocated in a way which will maximize the public good for the most residents possible. This is achieved through planned shrinkage. Policies should be enacted that creatively addresses the loss of population within these cities. This is achieved through targeted immigration policies. The haphazard planning currently demonstrated by many declining cities around targeted investments to certain businesses is at best ineffective and at worst wasteful of scarce resources.

## C. Where are the Feds?

The type of planning, reallocation of resources, and creative policies called for in *The Fiscal Cliff* are best addressed by the federal government. The federal government should have a vested interest in the success of our declining cities. After all, they helped to create them.

Many planners have argued that the abandonment by the federal government of urban areas since the 1960's has led to the state of many declining cities. The Federal-Aid Highway Act of 1956 allocated more than $26 billion to create 46,000 of interstate highways throughout the United States. President Eisenhower declared that the creation of a federal highway system was in the national interest of the United States. He argued that highways would allow people to exit cities quicker in case of a nuclear war. These highways also caused middle-class residents to flee to suburbs and exurbs when cities began to decline.

Many older, European cities also faced decline of their manufacturing capabilities after World War II. However, many cities remained viable because living in the suburbs was inconvenient. Paris is an excellent example of a European city with a burgeoning metropolis and decaying suburbs. Middle-class residents across Europe prefer living in the center of cities because transportation to the suburbs or exurbs is inconvenient.

The federal government also disinvested in the Department of Housing and Urban Development (HUD) which is the primary federal agency responsible for implementing urban policy. In the 1970's, HUD shifted tenant selection policy in federal housing projects and allowed the overconcentration of very low-income families in these developments. Many experts argue that this change in policy created the disastrous conditions that many public housing developments are in today. In the 1980's, the Reagan administration cut essential programs such as Section 8 housing and the Community Development Block Grant Programs which were programs essential to the creation of new housing and investment in urban neighborhoods.

By now, you've read and hopefully learned a great deal of the poor condition of declining cities. You've also read about how the lack of resources in declining cities inhibits these cities from addressing problems that impact its citizens such as public safety, public health and education. The solutions advocated in *The Fiscal Cliff* are aggressive solutions that require creative policies and long term planning. In order to change the status quo currently faced by declining cities, the federal government must become more involved.

In Chapter 4, we described how targeted immigration could help increase the population of declining cities and potentially increase the economic base of these cities through business development and job creation. Targeted immigration can only be implemented by the federal government. The Obama Administration, similar to the Bush Administration, is mired in the current status quo of federal immigration policy. By many estimates, there are 11 million illegal immigrants in the United States. A central question of any new immigration policy is how to grant citizenship to illegal immigrants currently in the United States without incentivizing their illegal activities or incentivizing foreigners to gain access to the United States illegally in order to earn their citizenship.

Targeted immigration provides an answer to these questions while providing a possible solution for declining cities. The federal government could require illegal immigrants to live in a declining city for five years in order to gain their citizenship. The city would benefit from the increase in population while immigrants would provide a useful service to the country by improving the futures of these cities. After all, immigration helped transform New York City into a leading global city. Imagine if the federal government recognized and harnessed the power of immigration to assist other declining cities.

Planned shrinkage, another policy proposed in this book, is also best implemented by the federal government. Municipal governments lack the resources or political will to implement this policy. Obviously, municipal governments will need to guide and inform the process. However, the reallocation of resources necessary for planned shrinkage cannot be done by municipalities alone. The federal government, through its police powers and ability to raise debt in the capital markets, possesses the regulatory tools and the capital market to truly transform cities.

Let's revisit Youngstown, OH and how the federal government's involvement could make a difference. Youngstown has probably embraced the concept of planned shrinkage more than any other city in the country. As we described earlier in Chapter 3, Youngstown has changed zoning within the city to accommodate for less density. The city has also identified certain neighborhoods as unsustainable and offered relocation assistance to any family willing to move from these neighborhoods. Finally, Youngstown has actively engaged the community through various outlets and multiple community meetings.

The largest deficiency in the plan is funding for relocation. The city is struggling to maintain its current budget and has cut funding for voluntary relocations. Without relocation, the city has been unable to cut services to neighborhoods which have been identified as unsustainable or create large blocks of vacant that can be used to attract small businesses, small manufacturers, or urban farms.

The federal government, or state government, could easily assist Youngstown in the continuation of its plan for relocation. The federal government could use eminent domain to pay for certain relocations from certain unsustainable neighborhood. The federal government could also guarantee tax incremental finance bonds to pay for relocation costs and incentive costs for the small businesses looking to relocate to the city into newly vacated blocks of land.

Another important attribute of the federal government is their political leverage. Mayors and city councilmembers typically run for their office every four years. Even if they win, term limits in certain cities may limit their stay in office to eight years. These municipal politicians, due to the nature of their office and the immediate needs of their constituencies, need to plan thoroughly for the short term and cannot spend time and resources planning for the long term. Mayor Richard Daley has served as mayor for Chicago from 1989 to 2010. Although I've mentioned that the majority of declining cities are in the Midwest and Northeast, Chicago has fared better than most Midwestern cities. Its downtown is thriving. Some of the success of Chicago must be attributed to the long tenure of its mayor.

The federal government can assist cities plan for the long term. And they must become more involved in addressing the problems affecting declining cities. They can devote resources to planning for a municipality 15 or 20 years out. The implementation of planned shrinkage, targeted immigration, or any other truly effective plan for declining municipalities must envision the city 10 to 20 years away. Planning until the next election cycle is not enough.

## D. Why Should You Care?

This is a book about people and places. Places influences people and people can recreate places. This book is also about structural changes, not marginal changes. It is about bold policy initiatives and a commitment to structural changes that will change places and allow a better quality of life for people. We, as Americans, can no longer accept the status quo within declining cities. The 13 million people that live in declining cities deserve better than substandard health care and decrepit public education facilities.

As a teenager in Harlem in the 1980's, I saw firsthand the impact a declining city can have. Crime was a constant concern. On my walks home from school, there was an open air drug market. Crack, cocaine, marijuana and PCP were easily available only two blocks from my elementary school. Drugs were not the only concern in my neighborhood. Muggings, robberies and homicides were also a constant concern. I was robbed of my bicycle, watch, and spending money before I turned 14.

My elementary school as a little boy was not much better. In the late 1970's, New York City had just averted a bankruptcy filing. Public schools were severely underfunded during the early 1980's. My elementary school could not purchase new textbooks or purchase pencils for the students. Children from three different grades shared the classroom and teacher because the school system could not afford to lower the teacher to student ratio from 1:32.

Why should you care? Remember, more than 13 million Americans live in declining cities. More than 13 million Americans are impacted by cities that have substandard public education or public safety institutions. America is a country of bold ideals and courageous people. And we are the wealthiest country in the world. There is no reason to allow so many American citizens to live with these substandard conditions if policies and strategies exist that can change their lives.

Why should you care? Because you can create a change in the way individuals and families are impacted by their cities. The greatest immigration boom ever in American history structurally changed New York City and altered the status quo. Population increased from 7 million in 1990 to 8.3 million in 2012. Immigrants transformed many downtrodden neighborhoods. They also provided labor, consumers and capital to businesses in the city.

Real change can happen for declining American cities. I've seen it. The status quo is an unacceptable way for any American citizen to live. I should know. I lived it. The policies in The Fiscal Cliff can make of difference in the lives of millions of Americans. But policies can only be implemented through advocates and supporters. I hope The Fiscal Cliff has made you an advocate for real change for declining American cities. Together, we can make a difference.

# ABOUT THE AUTHOR

Edward Poteat is a visionary urban planner and affordable housing developer. He was born and raised in Harlem during the crime epidemic of the 1980's and has devoted his life to social and economic equality issues in the urban environment. Edward is an adjunct professor of affordable housing at Columbia University and founded the Charles J. Poteat Fund which provides micro grants to community associations such as tenant associations and senior centers in Central Harlem.

Mr. Poteat is the Founder and President of Carthage Advisors, an affordable housing real estate firm that specializes in the redevelopment of older government subsidized properties in the New York City metropolitan area. The firm has approximately 1000 apartments in various stages of development and has exceptional expertise with devising sophisticated financial structures to rehabilitate existing affordable housing structures.

Mr. Poteat began his career as an Urban Fellow with the New York State Empire State Development Corporation. He received his undergraduate degree in Economics from Yale

University and received and Masters in Urban Planning from Hunter College.

Aside from development, Mr. Poteat holds or has held various board memberships or advisory board memberships with the Citizen Housing Planning Council, the New York City Housing Partnership, African-American Real Estate Professionals of New York, One Hundred Black Men and Urban Pathways. He has lectured about affordable housing on numerous industry panels and at several universities.

40460420R00117

Made in the USA
Middletown, DE
13 February 2017